Remixing the Curriculum

Remixing the Curriculum

The Teacher's Guide to Technology in the Classroom

Elizabeth Stringer Keefe
Adam Steiner

ROWMAN & LITTLEFIELD
Lanham • Boulder • New York • London

Published by Rowman & Littlefield
A wholly owned subsidiary of The Rowman & Littlefield Publishing Group, Inc.
4501 Forbes Boulevard, Suite 200, Lanham, Maryland 20706
www.rowman.com

Unit A, Whitacre Mews, 26-34 Stannary Street, London SE11 4AB

British Library Cataloguing in Publication Information Available

Library of Congress Cataloging-in-Publication Data

Names: Keefe, Elizabeth Stringer, 1972- author. | Steiner, Adam, 1973- author.
Title: Remixing the curriculum : the teacher's guide to technology in the classroom / Elizabeth Stringer Keefe, Adam Steiner.
Description: Lanham : Rowman & Littlefield, a wholly owned subsidiary of The Rowman & Littlefield Publishing Group, Inc., [2018] | Includes bibliographical references and index.
Identifiers: LCCN 2017047115 (print) | LCCN 2017058501 (ebook) | ISBN 9781475815719 (electronic) | ISBN 9781475815696 (cloth : alk. paper) | ISBN 9781475815702 (pbk. : alk. paper)
Subjects: LCSH: Educational technology.
Classification: LCC LB1028.3 (ebook) | LCC LB1028.3 .K432 2018 (print) | DDC 371.33—dc23 LC record available at https://lccn.loc.gov/2017047115

Printed in the United States of America

To Mom, Dad, and Jess
—ESK

To Kerry and my parents
—ACS

Contents

Foreword

This book is arriving just as a digital shift is underway in schools, a shift away from a teacher-centered delivery of a "one-size-fits-all" curriculum to one that is activity centered, wherein students engage with flexible media and materials, collaborate on projects with meaning and purpose, and make progress according to individual strengths. To guide teachers and school leaders through this transformation, Elizabeth Stringer Keefe and Adam Steiner have leveraged their years of teaching experience and professional preparation to propose what they call the "X framework."

It is particularly gratifying that their interest in universal design for learning (UDL) first emerged as part of a UDL leadership colloquium that I led at Boston College in the summer of 2011, as they were beginning their doctoral work. That initial inspiration has carried through their subsequent professional careers and is also an essential thread in this book, the culmination of years of study and their combined expertise in special education and technology.

Remixing the Curriculum and the X framework represent their experiences as both practitioners and researchers, and they are designed to accelerate access to the curriculum while creating unique learning conditions for all. At the center of the X framework is the intersection of four aspects of best practice: technology fitness, proactive planning, universal design for learning, and assistive technology.

By technology fitness the authors are referring to a mind-set or recognition that the media and tools of technology are forever evolving, requiring an ongoing readiness to match technologies with functional requirements. By proactive planning, the benefits of knowing in advance the needs and challenges of all learners is highlighted. With universal design for learning, a flexible curriculum wherein multiple options for presenting content, creating products, and relating to other learners is envisioned. Finally, with assistive technologies, the unique requirements of students with disabilities can be accommodated.

The X framework arrives at a particularly opportune time. Amid rapid technological change, an increasingly diverse student population, and a mandate for all students to access and participate in the general education curriculum, teachers and school leaders at all stages of development need inspiration, encouragement, and guidance. The idea that use of technology is today a lifestyle that must be embraced and incorporated into one's day-to-day activity is key to keeping pace with almost daily developments.

Proactive planning allows educators to be responsive to need rather than reactive to the inevitable problems that occur too late for resolution. Universal design for learning ensures a flexible curriculum to widen participation for all learners, and assistive technology enables access to learning for the most challenged students with special needs. The X framework provides not only an abundance of practical resources, but perhaps more important, a disposition for self-regulated ongoing professional learning.

Dr. Richard Jackson
Associate Professor, Lynch School of Education
Boston College
Chestnut Hill, Massachusetts

Acknowledgments

We wish to thank many people for their support, beginning with our patient spouses, Dennis Keefe and Kerry Dunne, and our children, Lucy, Cam, and Cooper Keefe and Nora and Maggie Steiner.

We are both indebted to Dr. Richard Jackson for his enthusiastic support and encouragement of this book, beginning with his guidance in the very first class we took as part of the Curriculum and Instruction PhD program at Boston College, where we met and began to collaborate. Additionally, we are grateful to both Dr. Marilyn Cochran-Smith and Dr. Andy Hargreaves for their support and mentoring, which helped shape us into the thinkers we are today.

We wish to acknowledge Liam Rutter Stokes for lending his artistic and all-around general expertise and support, especially in the final stages of the text; Liz Kenney Cox for her feedback and encouragement from the book's inception; and the many teacher colleagues and students we have worked with who motivated us to formalize our ideas.

And last, many thanks to our editor, Sarah Jubar, for her belief in this project and her enduring patience.

Part I

The Technology Mindset

You're in charge of your mind. You can help it grow by using it in the right way.

—Carol Dweck

Chapter One

The X Framework

Technology is nothing. What's important is that you have faith in people, that they're basically good and smart, and if you give them tools, they'll do wonderful things with them.

—Steve Jobs

There are few places more complex today than the K–12 classroom, a fact no one knows better than teachers. Our classrooms are comprised of a diverse fabric of students who vary educationally, racially, culturally, linguistically, and socioeconomically, and who each come through the door with a multitude of needs—many of which become the charge of the teacher. Add in the demands of curriculum, standardized assessment, and accountability reforms from critics of public education, and the result is a dizzying expectation for the educator.

Although societally we have recognized that the classroom has changed, it is teachers who have the very real and primary responsibility for shifting to address the change. Part of this involves developing and managing a rich and fluid academic environment that can support the needs of this vast array of learners. And as demands on public education increase—through education reform policies that hold teachers accountable for what students have or have not learned as the result of their instruction—the cost for teachers is that there is less time to plan, less time to refine, less space to work to meet the needs of many students at once.

Teachers have a choice at this juncture: try to teach so the majority of students benefit or undertake to create a curriculum as rich and diverse as the students before them. Since we know that the "traditional" student—an assumption based on the idea that there's a prototype student—is a myth, the first option hardly ever benefits anyone (students and teachers alike) because although students may be able to get by or manage instruction that's designed for the majority, it's not always optimal.

Today's classrooms are comprised of a baseline of all different kinds of learners who may sometimes learn in similar ways and at other times, not. Different learning circumstances may require different needs, even within individual students. We note here that we are avoiding use of the much-loved phrase, "learning styles," and though we leave the debate aside for brevity's sake, we offer as food for thought that this concept involves favoring student strengths, thus leaving areas of need somewhat unaddressed.

Instead, we suggest that the conditions under which we acquire new information are fluid and active and that students' needs shift by academic demand as a result. Thus, teachers must be continually adapting, changing, and shifting to meet the changing needs of students. These differences are the result of racially, culturally, linguistically, ethnically, and educationally diverse students representing a vast spectrum of different learning styles. Without expert, creative, and flexible teachers, meeting the needs of these learners would be next to impossible, leaving a quality education for *all* students in jeopardy.

The combination of a vast array of students' individual needs plus teachers' responsibility to ensure that these needs are met—all while managing demands related to pedagogy, curriculum, and assessment—creates a staggering breadth of need within the four walls of the "typical" classroom. When trying to meet these extensive needs, any student can be lost in the shuffle when the pace is fast.

Traditional approaches may fail to address the complex needs of some groups of students, such as students with disabilities, culturally and linguistically diverse students, and other at-risk students who may be unknowingly or unwittingly underserved, overlooked, underestimated, or even under-challenged. Teachers need a variety of options and supports—reliable, efficient and *inclusive* approaches—to balance classroom demands when traditional approaches fail. So how is this balance achieved? Most teachers already have many of the tools within their reach.

THE XFW

As we began working on this book, our individual beliefs, practices, and ideas came together to form what we refer to as the X framework, or XFW. As we considered the needs, challenges, and demands that educators encounter inside and outside of the classroom, we began to construct a framework comprised of four aspects of best practice that, when employed collectively, we believe accelerate access to the curriculum and create unique learning conditions under which to engage students.

We call this the X framework, because we believe that solutions to the aforementioned challenges occur at the *X*—the intersection of the following four aspects of teacher practice: technology fitness, proactive teaching, universal design for learning, and assistive technology (see figure 1.1).

Think of XFW as shifting in the same way that teacher practice naturally shifts to address students' different learning needs and styles. There is not necessarily an equal division of how the four aspects are used; rather, it is the incorporation of all four into conscious teaching practice that produces "X."

What is X, exactly? It's the intersection of self-reflective teaching and the opening where all students—those with different learning needs, approaches, differences, and backgrounds—have increased opportunity to access the curriculum, demonstrate their competence, and move beyond perceived obstacles to learning. It's about creating a classroom condition that supports all learners and provides a carefully constructed (yet realistic-to-achieve) opening for students to demonstrate their educational competence.

Applying this framework means reconsidering whether your practices match your beliefs. This is a difficult question for teachers to ask themselves but an absolutely necessary one that promotes growth and subtle readjustment of practice to ensure that it remains aligned with beliefs. For example, as a teacher, what do you say you believe in? Do your teaching practices match those beliefs?

In our work with teachers we often illustrate this concept using recycling as an example. When we ask a roomful of educators if they believe in recycling, many, if not all, raise their hands. But when asked to keep their hands raised if they did *not* throw away a recyclable this month, this week, or that day, we see a change. This is not an exercise designed to shame teachers

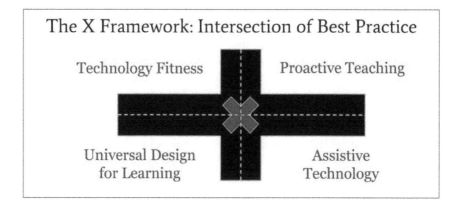

The X Framework: Intersection of Best Practice

Technology Fitness   Proactive Teaching

Universal Design
for Learning   Assistive
Technology

Figure 1.1.   Elizabeth Stringer Keefe

about their recycling practices, but rather to illustrate that practice can shift from beliefs without regular self-evaluation.

We believe that use of the XFW improves teacher practice overall by making it increasingly active, more engaging, and, most importantly, truly inclusive. Teachers working to incorporate these four aspects into their practice may worry less about "accommodations" for students who cannot access the traditional curriculum, may witness improved flexibility with regard to curriculum implementation, and may find collaboration with the team of professionals who work in classrooms and schools on behalf of our students much easier.

Despite our objection to education reforms such as value-added measures and narrowing of the curriculum through demands for testing—reforms often driven by hidden political agendas and implemented under less than desirable conditions, usually lacking teachers' voices—we do acknowledge that utilizing these practices will help teachers to address the expectations of such reforms, such as the Common Core Standards.

However, utilizing these practices in service of XFW helps increase teacher agency, in spite of external demands (such as education reforms) that drive the classroom. We define teacher agency as the deliberate acts of teachers to develop and cultivate their own professional growth, relying on their own expertise, training, and experience. This positions the teacher as expert and central to the classroom and the learners, rather than the victim of regulatory reforms and external influences.

We would love to be able to say it's an easy undertaking to shift in this way and convince teachers to give this a try. But as educators ourselves, we know that no matter which way you approach it, teaching requires presence, strength, and resilience, and it is *never* easy. We suggest here, then, that shifting practice, although a challenge, can help to achieve the desired results of learning in a positive and rewarding way, engaging for both student and teacher. It can also help you avoid the reactive nature of trying to support learners after the fact.

Although we cannot promise that it will be easy, we believe that the flexibility that results from the use of the X framework will elevate possibilities and improve outcomes for all students without feeling overwhelming. In this way, X becomes a *fulcrum*—the point "on which a lever rests or is supported, and on which it pivots" (Oxford Dictionaries, n.d.)—for access to the curriculum: technology fitness (TF) + proactive teaching (PT) + universal design for learning (UDL) + assistive technology (AT) = X.

Figure 1.2 illustrates how a fulcrum works. Quite simply, a fulcrum is a lever that when used correctly significantly multiplies the amount of effort exerted by the user. For example, to lift and balance a large and heavy object (such as a boulder, as pictured below), the user relies on the fulcrum to assist in moving the great weight of the boulder with a simple setup. Therefore, a heavier load can be moved with the use of the fulcrum than by the user alone. We've intentionally added an X within the fulcrum pictured in figure 1.2 to connect our concept of XFW to that of the fulcrum. Just as a heavier load can be moved using the fulcrum than can be moved by the user alone, we suggest that the opening created by XFW can serve as a fulcrum to create curricular access by utilizing the intersection of the four aspects of best practice rather than a singular effort on the part of the teacher alone.

Finding the intersection of all four of these aspects of teaching might sound daunting, but the truth is, you're probably already doing more than you think. We suggest that it's thinking about marrying all four of these aspects of practice that will accelerate student access and growth. Below, we introduce the four aspects of XFW; their uses in the classroom are detailed in subsequent chapters.

Technology fitness (TF) is a concept we developed to describe digital technology "fitness," wherein we outline other ways that teachers, students, classrooms, and districts can achieve a healthy balance of technology and flexible learning. The most obvious meaning of the word *fitness* refers to health and physical condition, but it also relates to competence and ability to fulfill a task.

Our thinking on technological fitness evolved from our own innate understanding of these two meanings together, as we thought about how technology could be best utilized in the classroom. Therefore, technology fitness relates to a measure of not just how technology is used, but also how it is regarded by the teacher, including the educator's own perceptions of preparedness to use it (we discuss measuring and tracking your own TF in chapter 2).

Just like physical fitness, technology fitness can be continually improved and is best served when a complete approach is taken, meaning that teachers

Figure 1.2. Liam Rutter-Stokes

evaluate their baseline fitness. This begins with an evaluation of their level of comfort using it and of how well it is being used in the classroom. TF is also a way for teachers and school leaders to gauge their technology curricula, decisions, and ongoing education. TF also provides a basis for educators to evaluate the quality of and capacity for effective use of technology to improve student learning.

Proactive teaching (PT) is a simple concept but requires a shift in thinking, practice, and behavior. We have intentionally used a simple concept to demonstrate what we believe is a complex aspect of effective practice. Proactive teaching is a way to frontload the work of reaching all learners prior to the major instruction, rather than managing (reactively) the areas where students fall short or need additional support following instruction.

Most teachers begin this through the planning process. The way we think about proactive teaching draws on the concept of adaptive teaching, particularly as conceptualized by Corno (2008), who theorized it as a way for teachers to address student differences related to learning by responding to learners as they work. Teachers read student signals to diagnose needs on the fly and tap previous experience with similar learners to respond productively.

Adaptive teaching requires teachers to use their experience and expertise to develop efficiency and innovation in teaching, two dimensions that Hammerness and colleagues (2005) viewed as critical for teachers to reflect their ability to balance innovation, knowledge, and "diagnostic and instructional" skills for educating students who require "different approaches or additional supports" (p. 360).

Proactive teaching, therefore, requires teacher understanding of a complex process that includes "characteristics of learners, the acquisition and transfer of knowledge, the critical role of environments and the role of assessment in guiding learning" (De Arment, Reed, & Wetzel, 2013, p. 218). Adaptive expertise requires a teacher to utilize innovation in curriculum and problem solving as opposed to gravitating toward known or familiar interventions or approaches, a critical tenet of adopting the best practices that comprise the X framework.

Universal design for learning (UDL), a philosophy of teaching and learning that provides teachers with the guideposts to respond to the fluid learning needs of students, focuses on the what, how, and why of learning through a framework utilizing three brain networks: recognition, strategic, and affective (CAST, 2011).

The philosophy of UDL dictates that the differences that students bring to learning is "as varied and unique as our DNA or fingerprints" and thus, in order to truly benefit from the curriculum, students must have exposure to information and content that is presented in different ways, opportunities to express their knowledge, and a continuous focus on the motivation and engagement of learning.

UDL is one of the four aspects of XFW that requires an adjustment of practice—primarily in our approach to the way we think about learning. To make such a shift, teachers must separate true student learning goals from the means by which these goals are attained (CAST, 2011). This requires relinquishing teaching methods of the past in favor of flexibility, creativity, and variability—the pillars of our new understanding of what is absolutely necessary for all students to learn and thrive in today's classrooms. Chapter 3 details proactive teaching and the principles of the UDL network.

Assistive technology (AT) is defined as "any item, piece of equipment, or product system, whether acquired commercially off the shelf, modified, or customized, that is used to increase, maintain, or improve the functional capabilities of a child with a disability" (Individuals with Disabilities Education Act, 2004, sec. 300.5).

AT is required by law for students with disabilities and is a way to ensure student success in the general education classroom by providing students with the tools to access the curriculum. This is good for teachers, too, since these supports are good not only for the student who needs them, but for the rest of the students in the class as well.

Finally, with the infusion of technology into our society, these technology supports are often seamless, meaning they are everyday items, programs, or tools that many people use, so they do not single out students in the classroom.

ORGANIZATION OF THE BOOK

The ten chapters in this book are divided into two parts with five chapters each. The book is organized to help advance an educator's thinking about the four aspects of the X framework, for which we provide explanations below.

Part I: The Technology Mindset details what is required of the educator to shift to the use of technology in the classroom. In chapter 2, we delve deeply into evaluating technology fitness as a form of teacher agency, elaborating on the concept of technology fitness to illustrate how "fitness" must extend to the classroom to allow for self-reflection of practice and continual reevaluation of the four aspects of XFW. Chapter 3 details proactive teaching and the primary networks of the UDL philosophy.

In chapter 4, we guide you through the differences between classroom and assistive technology and discuss alignment to the UDL principles that match the content and offer teachers choices in their instructional approach. The final chapter in part I, chapter 5, provides an overview of shifts in school culture that have occurred as the result of technology.

Part II of the book, Remixing the Classroom, provides specific methodologies that teachers can use to represent curriculum in varied ways to address the needs of their diverse learners and implement technology in the classroom. Each of the chapters in this section is designed to provide educators with unique applications of digital and assistive technology that are free or low cost, easy to use, and readily available to help them meet the diverse needs of the students in their classrooms.

Chapter 6 provides an overview of some foundational technologies that are free, easy to use, and likely already within reach, describing technology as a "classroom pillar" and a complement to traditional approaches, where technology becomes a vehicle to access rather than a burden.

Chapter 7 describes the next generation of the lecture, offering examples of digital technology that serve as levers for providing access to the curriculum and a brief explanation of the benefits to the classroom, the teacher, and the student. This chapter describes shifting the "sage on the stage" model to one transformed into an updated, collaborative, engaging form of teaching and learning, where instead of merely lecturing, the educator facilitates the active participation of students.

Chapter 8 discusses emerging trends that may propel school and classroom technology into an entirely new realm. The chapter focuses on a relatively new but increasingly embraced educational concept, maker education, a term posited by Dale Dougherty (2012) that describes a collaborative, hands-on learning approach to authentic problem solving. This chapter is also a foray into "gamification"—the adaptation of video games into education.

We thought this was a critically important chapter to include because the concept of gaming in education brings play squarely back into the picture. Scholars and researchers have long lamented the dwindling existence of learning through play in favor of structure and testing and standards, and we think gamification offers a unique opportunity to revisit how closely learning and play are related.

Chapter 9 is dedicated to helping educators support their students to "show what they know" and reviews both digital technologies and ways to enhance literacy, a content area that spans the entire curriculum and offers technology as a way to bring it to life for students for whom it has been inaccessible in the past. This chapter offers a variety of options for helping students to demonstrate understanding through novel, easy to use, and engaging technologies that don't alter the curricular expectation, but rather the path to achieving it.

Finally, the book concludes with a suggestion that using the XFW is more about "repurposing" practice than changing it. We reinforce the expert role of the teacher and offer ways to consider ongoing reflective practice using Technology Fitness in an effort to extend repurposing practice using the XFW. We propose that this approach enhances teacher agency and honors teacher expertise.

Chapter Two

Technology Fitness

Quality is much better than quantity. One home run is better than two doubles.
—Steve Jobs

We've come a long way since the first computer. For many years, technology was for the elite—expensive, mysterious, and unattainable (partly because of its bulk! Who can erase from their memories the photos of the gigantic computers that took up half of a room?). Today, it's a very different story: not only is technology more accessible, but it's rare to see people in public who *aren't* visibly engaged with—or at least carrying—digital devices. Technology has a fixed place in our daily lives: it's how most of us stay connected to loved ones, access the news, enjoy entertainment, fulfill work obligations, maintain our calendars, make shopping lists, and check the weather. It's safe to say that technology is no longer for the elite; technology enhances or improves daily life for more people than ever before.

One critically important aspect of this evolution is the decline of the "digital divide"—a term that has been used to describe the gap between economic resources and access to technology that can essentially be attributed to demographics, class, and income level (Norris, 2001). Research suggests that technology accessibility for those living below the poverty level has been improving continually, which helps to characterize technology as an educational tool that can have a place in the classroom now and in the future, with less concern about creating a tiered system whereby students with resources have access but others may not.

For example, the US Census Bureau reported that in 2011 81 percent of households living below the poverty level had cell phones with Internet access and nearly 60 percent of households had a computer (File, 2013). The U.S. Impact Study reported in 2015 that 85 percent of users reported having

11

regular personal access to a computer and the Internet somewhere other than the library. This means that many people access the Internet in a variety of ways.

A 2015 Pew report suggested that 87 percent of adults use the Internet, and a whopping 68 percent of them do so by connecting with their mobile devices (Perrin, 2015). But even more interesting is that 91 percent of teens access the Internet from their mobile devices (Lenhart, 2015). There's some controversy about whether this fact is good or bad for teens, but either way, regular access to the Internet indicates a change in our overall technological saturation. For this reason, we suggest that the decline in the digital divide is related not to the physical "what" of technology—what you own, what you have access to—but rather *how* technology is used.

TECHNOLOGY IN SCHOOLS: ASSET OR LIABILITY?

As we allude to earlier, despite our improved access to technology as a whole, there remains some controversy about it—especially regarding its use in educational settings. In fact, a 2017 survey conducted by Project Tomorrow indicated that 67 percent of technology leaders indicated that the greatest barrier to implementing technology in schools was "motivating teachers to change their instructional practices to use technology more meaningfully with students." We suggest this challenge is not solely related to teachers' unwillingness, but rather to a variety of factors: varying opinions about appropriateness and effectiveness; teacher's understanding of, interest in, and comfort level using technology; and overall district, school, and teacher technology activity and support.

One of the biggest dilemmas regarding the use of technology in schools regards the ethics of technology use, which we want to address up front. As our society begins to rely more and more on technology in daily life, trepidation exists that the teaching emphasis in classrooms and schools will shift from the guidance of an expert teacher to overreliance upon technology.

Our position is that no technology can or will ever replace a skilled teacher, and we do not support any practice, theory, or organization that suggests this. To reinforce this, we propose three priorities as the rationale for the use of technology in schools: (1) technology can be an asset to the expertise of the teacher through thoughtful pedagogical decisions, especially when carefully aligned with curricular foci and learner profiles; (2) technology saturates our society, and schools must take the lead in modeling its ethical use for students; and finally (3) technological saturation in society can mean more inclusive spaces wherein those who use technology for access and communication, such as students with disabilities, and those who use technology for convenience, organization, or fun, can operate on a more level playing field. These factors, and our observations of technology in use (or collecting dust!) in educational settings, helped us to conceive the concept we introduced in chapter 1: technology fitness (TF).

The most recognized meaning of *fitness* relates to health and physical condition, and we pause on that a moment here to unpack the reason why we chose this term. As a society, we place enormous emphasis on health, or "fitness." There's an important societal phenomenon related to fitness—a continual emphasis on overall health, including good food choices and exercises, much of which is framed in the service of longevity. Within this, there are many different philosophies and practices and levels of commitment, but overall, physical fitness is highly personal and highly individual.

Physical fitness begins with an evaluation of self, behavior, and practices and builds slowly as people make small changes that eventually lead to more substantive ones that help them to sustain their physical condition over time. To this end, we see a parallel between the concept of physical fitness and technology fitness. We believe teachers can improve their comfort level using technology by evaluating their technological sense in a similar way, beginning with an evaluation of self, including identifying their stances on technology and how it affects instructional practices. Much like the trajectory toward good health, building technological confidence slowly by making small changes clears the path to greater classroom engagement with technology. In part, this is because fitness has another meaning, which is "relating to competence and ability to fulfill a task." These two definitions taken together make technology fitness highly personal and achievable according to what is comfortable for the user rather than trying to meet a specific standard or expectation.

When teachers are asked to change or shift their technological practice, it's often linked to innovation and advancement but not always founded in clear and specific understanding of learner development and theoretical and pedagogical knowledge, a fact we think frustrates teachers, who rightly resist. Technology fitness was born of our personal and collective experiences as university-prepared public school educators who have taught in a variety of settings and held a variety of roles in schools. Since evaluating technology fitness requires reflection about practice, we thought it was important to make evident that this was developed with firsthand knowledge of the demands and expectations that teachers feel on a daily basis.

GETTING TECHNOLOGICALLY FIT

In light of the pressures we know teachers face in the classroom managing critics, reformers, assessments, data—*before* even getting to the biggest responsibility of the classroom: the learners!—we began to think of how educators could reflect upon, think about, gauge, and exercise their own techno-logical knowledge, activity, confidence, and willingness. The result of this exercise, through self-inventory and reflection, can be used as a way to help teachers identify where they currently are with regard to technology use in their teaching, target areas for growth and improvement, and create a person-alized plan to enact technology goals. Given the dynamic, fluid, and active work teachers engage in, we again draw a parallel to the concept of physical fitness. Physical fitness relies on many components—healthful body compo-sition, healthful eating, cardiovascular and muscular endurance, strength, and flexibility. Physical activity also matters to overall fitness—how often and how well you move. Although there are complexities to physical fitness beyond this basic description, it is a useful analogy to help educators consid-er their own technology use in teaching and potentially as a way for schools and districts to gauge decision making about technology resources.

Borrowing from the ways in which the components of physical fitness interact, we began to think about how this concept could be applied to teach-ers and their education. Drawing on Shulman's (1986) research on teacher pedagogical content knowledge (PCK), which was the first to suggest that a teacher's knowledge and practice were highly connected (rather than mutual-ly exclusive), we developed components of technology fitness to honor the interactions among several complex factors. In addition, we harnessed as-pects of a later variation of PCK, technological pedagogical content knowl-edge (TPCK) (Mishra & Koehler, 2006), to expand the components of tech-nology fitness.

There are five components of technology fitness, all of which are interre-lated, though not necessarily hierarchical:

1. tech knowledge
2. tech consumption
3. tech effectiveness
4. tech motivation
5. tech activity (see figure 2.1)

Just like physical fitness, technology fitness can be improved continually and is best served when a complete approach is taken, meaning that teachers evaluate their own baseline fitness. This begins with an evaluation of each of the areas of TF to determine how and why technology is being used in the classroom.

For the purpose of this book, we use the concept of TF as it relates to teachers, but we also believe the concept can be applied to students, class-rooms, schools, and entire districts. Technology can be a useful reference as teachers and school leaders try to gauge how technology aligns with their curricula, decisions, purchases, and ongoing professional development. TF

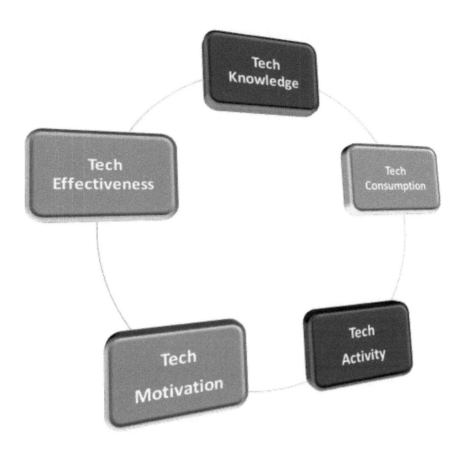

Figure 2.1.   Elizabeth Stringer Keefe

can help teachers achieve a healthy balance of technology and flexible learning in their own classrooms. TF is also a way for teachers and school leaders to assess their technology curricula, decisions, and ongoing education, and it provides a basis for educators to evaluate the quality of and capacity for effective use of technology to improve student learning. As teachers and school leaders reflect on technology fitness, it can assist them in capitalizing on current resources, in assessing the efficiency of the use of particular resources, and in targeting areas for growth.

THE FIVE COMPONENTS OF TECHNOLOGY FITNESS

Developing an understanding of the five components of tech fitness is essential to evaluating personal tech fitness. Below we outline the components.

Tech knowledge is the scope of what a teacher knows about technology, and it's important to remember that this knowledge is not fixed; rather it is ever changing and moving. Mishra and Koehler (2006), who created technological pedagogical content knowledge (TPACK), a newer conceptualization of PCK, suggested that technology should be added to the PCK framework, given the rapid evolution of digital technology and the fact that "teaching is a highly complex activity that draws on many kinds of knowledge" (p. 1020).

Mishra & Koehler (2006) define tech knowledge as the knowledge of more traditional technologies that have a permanent place in schools (books, blackboards, whiteboards) as well as emerging digital technology. Their concept of learning and adapting as technology changes is critical. They suggest that since technology is continually changing, instead of teaching "fixed" technology skills, the nature of technological knowledge must shift with emerging digital technology, otherwise those fixed skills will be related to technology that disappears as quickly as it arrives. But as Mishra and Koehler posit, "the ability to learn and adapt to new technologies (irrespective of what the specific technologies are) will still be important" (p. 1027–28).

The authors' astute predictions about evolving technology are relevant today. Consider that the first iPhone, released in 2007, sold more than one million phones within months and just ten years later has morphed from a phone into a personal digital cache, holding music, credit cards, plane tickets, health stats, and more. Incorporating the changing nature of technology is absolutely necessary for thinking about personal tech knowledge. Since we developed the concept of technology fitness to specifically facilitate self-reflection about readiness for technology use, we define tech knowledge as both the scope of a teacher's knowledge about standard technologies and the *ability to learn new technology*. Possessing only technical skills can lead to a struggle with developing and expanding learning, so tech knowledge must incorporate developing skills, which will give teachers the confidence to approach or deconstruct a new technology.

Tech knowledge is not fixed, and it is specific to the user. Thus it can be simple, from a basic understanding of today's technologies—cell phones, use of e-mail—to vast, for example, knowledge of the protocol used to regulate the majority of Internet traffic. One critical aspect of how we define tech knowledge that differentiates our definition from that of previous conceptions is that technology knowledge, however sophisticated, does not necessarily correlate to increased technology consumption or technology activity. Think again of physical fitness to understand this analogy: one may have extensive understanding of the importance of healthy eating and exercise yet may still be overweight and/or sedentary. A teacher may have extensive knowledge of technology but be unwilling or unable to use it in the classroom for a variety of reasons (lack of resources, lack of support, trepidation about its usefulness, etc.).

We refer to technology consumption as the sum of technology a teacher uses—both the kinds/types of technology use in any realm and the technology that they personally own. Consumption is sometimes defined as "the purchase of and use of goods and services by the public" (Oxford Dictionary, n.d.). Consumption is an easy concept to extend to technology. It's very simply an inventory of what you have, what you use, and how. The first level of inventory is personal tech consumption. Technology use in daily life, such as computer, Internet, and cell phone use may seem irrelevant to an overall appraisal of tech use in a professional realm, but our personal ownership of technology has true bearing on how, why, and with what frequency technology is used in the educator's professional role. This aspect of tech fitness also speaks to a sea change with regard to personal technology use: in 2011, 35 percent of Americans reported owning a smartphone, but in 2016, that number rose to 77 percent (Smith, 2017).

Tech consumption is important to consider because personal use of technology can help forecast a teacher's comfort level in trying new technologies in the classroom (tech motivation) and then implementing and using technology (tech activity). Teachers may not necessarily relate their personal use of technology to how it could benefit their instruction in the classroom, but taking an inventory might connect the two. Consider these questions:

- What technology do I personally own (phone, calculator, computer, TV, DVR, video camera, satellite radio, automatic car starter, keyless door entry, GPS, etc.)?
- What technology do I have access to professionally (computers, digital notebooks, smartboards, clickers, Internet, cloud storage, iPads, e-readers, etc.)?
- What technology do I personally use on a daily basis, in both personal and professional realms (Internet, social media, e-mail, apps, etc.)?

There are many times when technology use is not a choice, but rather the result of its ubiquitous influence in our culture. For example, consider the disappearance of pay phones, landlines, records, and tapes, whose existences were neutralized by their digital counterparts. Things become obsolete much more rapidly than they used to—remember the rise (and fall) of the portable GPS? That technology was quickly replaced by apps on cell phones that eradicated the need for separate devices. The important thing to note is that these cultural shifts in technology use can be otherwise unaccounted for when determining overall personal consumption. However, after thinking it through in this way, teachers who might otherwise describe themselves as tech novices may have more experience than they think. Conducting an inventory can increase confidence to infuse new technology into practice in the classroom.

Technology activity (or "techercise") is a measure of how often (or how much) technology is used. This draws heavily on the concept of physical fitness. The first step in gauging overall health is determining your level of activity, usually categorized as "sedentary," "low active," "active," or "very active." For ease, we use these same labels, since many people already have a common understanding of what they mean and what that activity level entails. However, we've shifted the activity to focus specifically on technology:

- *Sedentary* use involves typical but minimal daily technology activity (using a cell phone, checking e-mail, sending a text, watching television). Technology use is somewhat restricted and limited.
- *Low active* use refers to sedentary activity plus additional technology use that helps to provide access to information beyond what is specific to the user (active Internet use, including surfing, reading news online, digital music, use of digital apps for games and amusement).
- *Active* technology use refers to low activities plus additional technology action that involves application and extension of the technology for broader reach to a bigger arena (use of chat and video messaging, use of one or more popular social media sites, such as Facebook, Twitter, Instagram, etc.).
- *Very active* use includes all previous activities, plus vigorous technology use in most or all aspects of professional life. Very active use may involve a "social footprint," which gauges use and activity of social media.

Most people can quickly and easily categorize themselves into one of those levels. As we mentioned before, the important thing to remember is that "techercise" has very little to do with knowledge. You many know quite a bit about technology but choose not to use it. We think that tenet alone is something that is overlooked when considering teachers' technology use. For example, you may be able to navigate an online banking site easily but choose to use more traditional methods to pay bills, which may be more a reflection of personal beliefs and perceptions than of understanding. "Techercise" simply gauges the amount of tech activity; the next category, technology motivation, helps to identify what influences decisions with regard to activity.

Motivation is a concept that is often explored and referred to in education, particularly as it relates to student learning. A basic assumption about motivation is that it is what gets you started and must involve effort and likely hard work. A deeper assumption is that motivation is related to willingness, desire, and enthusiasm for a task. We define *tech motivation* as the factors that influence your technology use—such as personal beliefs and perceptions (such as views about the appropriateness of technology use for curricular access), access to technology (interest in the use of technology but it is not readily available), and comfort level in using technology. Along those lines, *technology risk* also influences motivation—a general willingness to try technology new to you or not before using it in the classroom. For example, would you attempt to learn how to use a smartboard if there was one available, even if you have had no training or previous experience with the technology?

One final aspect of technology motivation is the array of learners that you teach. This is a critical aspect not only of tech motivation, but also of technology fitness and the X framework in general. Differences in a classroom population of learners from year to year make it necessary for any teacher to shift their expertise to successfully reach each student and respond to their individual needs—a daunting task. Although individualized instruction is usually not possible in today's classrooms, technology can assist teachers in moving beyond traditional methods that might exclude learners from accessing and benefitting from the curriculum and the classroom community. So, diversity in learners, especially those with disabilities, can be a significant motivator for teacher technology use.

Technology effectiveness is essentially the application of technology in practice. This is the final step, and the point at which a teacher can make decisions about how to translate knowledge, consumption, activity and motivation into use. This is not necessarily the place where the process shifts from thinking to action, but rather the place in the process to reflect on how well specific technology is aligned with aspects of teaching practice. This is the place to differentiate the effective use of technology from the use of technology for technology's sake. For example, we don't have tablets in the classroom because they are shiny and new and interesting—like all else, we need a clear curricular justification for their use. These might include expanding students' options for writing tasks, collaborating in real time on one digital document, using speech-to-text applications, or layering traditional text with images and sound.

To reflect on effectiveness, consider how efficient technology use is. This process is undertaken only after taking stock of tech knowledge, consumption, activity, and motivation, because like the previous four, this aspect of the process remains highly individual and is dependent on how the teacher has considered the previous four categories. Using that information, this step assists teachers in evaluating and aligning technology with their instruction. See table 2.1 for a list of questions designed to guide the process.

Technology effectiveness is relatively simple, but it represents the difference between using technology merely as a fun addition and using it to serve the purpose of overall academic achievement. Although the questions focus on students, it's in the service of helping teachers evaluate their own overall tech fitness and readiness to take small steps toward enhancing instruction with technology. It's important to note that the technology being considered

Table 2.1 *Evaluating Tech Effectiveness*

Nature of the curricular task	What does the teacher require of the students in the academic task, and how is it traditionally taught? What is the overall goal of learning? What are students expected to achieve during the process? What outcome will indicate that they have met the expectation?
Consideration of the student	What students may benefit from alternate means of instruction given their learning needs? Can other students benefit from choices in instructional trajectory? Does the technology represent an opportunity for students to be active participants in the learning process?
Choosing the technology	What technology stands out as supporting the goals of instruction? When a technology is identified, are there obvious reasons it has been chosen? Does it have a clear alignment to the instructional method or content? Does the technology require additional skills on the part of the student that may detract from, rather than enhance, the curricular goal?
Evaluating a technology	Is the technology a vehicle for access to the curriculum? Does the use of technology enhance the traditional method? Does the teacher feel comfortable using it, or is the teacher comfortable with tech risk? Will use of technology result in higher student engagement? Can technology equally represent or enhance the content? Does the technology provide students improved and multiple ways of demonstrating knowledge?
Measuring the outcome	What was the teacher's comfort level in implementing and using the tech? At the completion of the academic task, have students achieved the teacher's articulated goal of learning? Has the use of technology assisted students in achieving the same result, or has it significantly changed the outcome? Did students utilize the technology with ease, or did the technology require more support from the teacher than anticipated? What could be adjusted to support seamless tech use to better align with the teacher's instruction?

is taken from the choices generated by the teacher themselves in the previous steps of the process, so it can be an iPad for some, while a set of classroom clickers for others.

Avoiding the (Academic) New Year's Resolution Trap

Each September (give or take a few weeks) represents a new start for every teacher. It's the reset of the academic year and—much like New Year's Day—can represent an opportunity to redefine personal goals and activities that support identified and desired outcomes. But, as wonderful and hopeful as this sounds, a recent survey by Statistic Brain (2017) suggested that only 9 percent of people feel they are successful at their resolutions every year.

Instead of rushing into using technology in the classroom, we suggest that a slow and steady approach is more beneficial for developing comfort and for ultimately sustaining use. We offer the following advice for thinking about shifting practice fluidly and seeing results over time, which is more useful than expecting dramatic change overnight.

Start small. Developing your comfort level and an understanding stance about the use of technology is really the first and most important step. It involves recognition and desire for change, even if small. Begin by evaluating tech knowledge, which involves moving back and forth between the first three categories of tech fitness fluidly.

Make a list. Tech consumption and tech activity determine the basis for tech knowledge. Begin by considering tech consumption and list all technologies that have a place in daily life. Then consider what you know about each technology and how you learned it. To this end, the lists become a confidence-building task designed to demonstrate that average people have more technological skill than they realize.

Choose your tool. Determining your approach to use of personal technology provides important clues about how to parlay this into professional use. For example, what tools do we learn to use new phones? Is it trial and error? A tutorial from a trusted source? Reading the instructions? Watching videos online? Once the method has been determined, figure out how it can apply to new technologies that you may be interested in using, especially in the classroom.

Talk to your friends. Identify other teachers or professionals who are using technology in the school and align yourselves! Collaboration and networking often fall by the wayside when trying to manage the demands of the classroom, especially if they involve working together above and beyond the most obvious needs of students. Finding spaces and time to discuss tech options and what works and doesn't work for other educators is a great start in developing tech knowledge and increasing consumption and activity.

Try a pilot. You don't have to commit to permanent change, but experimenting with technology as a layer to instruction helps teachers to determine how to increase their activity slowly but surely. Trials can provide enormous information about confidence level, student response, alignment to task, and overall success (or disaster!). It's okay if things go poorly—sometimes we learn more from what didn't go well than from what did. Using small pilots and trials helps to build and develop overall teacher confidence for more systematic technology use.

Tech Fitness and the X Framework

Determining tech fitness is an essential aspect of applying the X framework in a classroom, but again, it's important to remember that tech fitness is both highly personal and fluid. It can change according to the teacher, the academic task, and the learning conditions. We emphasize the teacher as expert and offer tech fitness as a way to emphasize teacher agency—these choices are another way of cultivating professional growth through personal choices made at one's own pace.

Chapter Three

Proactive Teaching and Universal Design for Learning

Reforming education, improving schools, and raising student achievement are noble and socially just pursuits, but by what means are these lofty goals to be accomplished?

—Dr. Richard Jackson

ORGANIZING INSTRUCTION FOR (EVERYONE'S) SUCCESS

For a moment, reimagine the traditional curricular model: the very first priority for the teacher is a thoughtful inventory of student learning needs alongside the content, resulting in an intentionally designed method of instruction structured to remove any impediments or barriers that students might experience based on their individual learning needs. This is a "curricular remix," an idea for rethinking the approach to curriculum development that is borrowed from music. Think of a musical remix—a song that becomes different from its original form, retaining its basic foundational elements, but changing through additions or alterations to create a new version. Both are usually appealing, sometimes to different listeners. Remixing the curriculum works in the same way: using the essential elements of the original but redesigning it to offer an updated version with new features, which creates different learning opportunities and experiences and promotes access and engagement.

There are a variety of models of instruction in teaching, and they are not all static, meaning that teachers likely vary their instructional approach for different academic content and academic tasks. There is some content that is more traditionally aligned with different approaches and instructional groupings—for example, students are frequently grouped together for science content—but why? Is it because the content is best aligned for this kind of learning? Or perhaps it is driven by availability of materials and resources? How do teachers make instructional and grouping decisions, and how can this model be improved?

There are several stages of classroom teaching, but they can generally be broken down into four categories in more traditional models: planning, instruction, assessment, and support—each requiring specific actions on the part of the teacher. In the planning stage, teachers consider the content, prepare materials and learning activities designed to be the vehicle for learning, and determine the method for instruction. During instruction in a traditional model, the transfer of knowledge occurs from teachers via their chosen instructional method and the activities they have designed to support learning. In the assessment stage, teachers reflect on what parts of instruction need adjustment or could be improved by making pedagogical changes and identify where both the class as a whole and specific students might need additional support. The support stage (sometimes referred to as "classroom management") occurs partly during instruction but continues after instruction as well, when teachers attend to what they have diagnosed as needing adjustment. This stage may include clarifying students' questions, working with students who lag behind the pace of the majority, and responding to behaviors that interfere with instruction.

Instruction commonly occurs using these four stages because it's logical and it has helped teachers to know the extent to which their students have mastered specific content or a specific standard. So, the method of instruction is usually determined based on the type of content, learning is intended to occur during this instructional period, assessment determines the extent to which teachers have reached their instructional goals, and support is offered in response to assessment retrospectively and in vivo to students who cannot access the content in part or whole.

This model has longevity in schools partly due to tradition, partly due to efficiency (and the need to cover an enormous amount of curriculum), and partly due to the availability of resources. This may be the most organized way to approach instruction, but what would a remix additionally offer the teacher *and* the students? Could learning be more seamless for students if their needs were considered in concert with content, rather than after the design of delivery of the content? Could this model actually be more efficient for the teacher, even though it requires a shift from reactive to proactive?

In the previous chapter, the concept of technology fitness (TF) was introduced as a way to enact teacher agency around the use of technology in the classroom as the first aspect of the X framework (XFW). Below, two more quadrants of XFW are introduced: proactive teaching (PT) and universal design for learning (UDL). Proactive teaching is a simple concept but requires a shift in thinking, practice, and behavior.

UDL is a research-based set of principles for curriculum development, teaching, and learning that accounts for the diversity of learners in the classroom today and emphasizes instruction that aligns with the learning networks of the brain. These two important approaches, when used in concert with TF and assistive technology, described in chapter 4, create a significant educational opening to the curriculum, where more learning opportunities are available for the range of learning needs across the diverse classroom.

PROACTIVE TEACHING

Proactive teaching (PT) is a simple concept, utilized in XFW to demonstrate a complex and necessary aspect of effective teaching practice. Proactive teaching is the difference between frontloading the work of reaching all learners *prior* to the major instruction, versus reactively managing the areas in which students fall short or need additional support following instruction. Most teachers begin this through the planning process.

The way we think about proactive teaching draws on the concept of adaptive teaching, particularly as conceptualized by Corno (2008), who theorized it as a way for teachers to address student differences related to learning by responding to learners as they work. Teachers read student signals to diagnose needs on the fly and tap previous experience with similar learners to respond productively. Adaptive teaching and expertise require teachers to use their experience and expertise to develop efficiency and innovation in teaching, two dimensions that Hammerness and colleagues (2005) viewed as critical for teachers to reflect their ability to balance innovation, knowledge, and "diagnostic and instructional" skills for educating students who require "different approaches or additional supports" (p. 360).

Proactive teaching, therefore, requires teacher understanding of a complex process that includes "characteristics of learners, the acquisition and transfer of knowledge, the critical role of environments and the role of assessment in guiding learning" (De Arment, Reed, & Wetzel, 2013, p. 218). Adaptive expertise requires a teacher to utilize innovation in curriculum and problem solving as opposed to gravitating toward known or familiar interventions or approaches, a critical tenet of adopting the best practices that comprise the X framework.

Proactive teaching requires that teachers set the learning context to support the most optimal conditions for student learning. This may involve grouping and is worth exploration. Reconsider the myth of the "average" or "typical" student, which we referred to in chapter 1. Grouping students has long been an educational practice, and for as long as it has existed, it has been accompanied by professional dialogue and controversy. We know now that although grouping often happens as a reflexive part of teaching, some instructional groupings can be beneficial, such as cooperative learning approaches, described earlier, whereas others, such as grouping students by perceived "ability," are not and can help to perpetuate the "typical student" myth and unfairly limit the potential of students.

One way to consider grouping students is by learning approach or learning needs, which is a more natural process. However, groupings must also be fluid and active, as students may have different learning needs that relate to different content. One example is the cooperative learning approach (Johnson & Johnson, 1999) in which students work in small groups on a common task. In this model, the idea is that students benefit both individually and as a group through working together to accomplish a shared goal. In this way, students contribute individually but are accountable to other group members, and as a result the students work together to maximize both their individual learning and each other's (Johnson & Johnson, 1999).

One of the original concepts of cooperative learning was that students of varying abilities would be grouped together. There's no doubt that at any given time in the classroom, there are varying abilities, but a progressive way to think about it is that this is true of all tasks. It may be that students bring particular strengths to some tasks and challenges to others. This model allows teachers to support students by identifying where they can be leaders and also where they may have the opportunity to improve their skills in a supportive space. Thus, this kind of instructional grouping (and other models like it) is an example of proactive teaching. When instruction is considered in this way, the myth of the "average" or "traditional" student is further dispelled.

Proactive teaching also involves organization, though it is not limited to this, of course. This means being prepared for how students may respond to certain academic tasks and having the appropriate supports ready; establishing student roles in conjunction with academic learning so they are active participants; and identifying aspects of the academic expectations in advance that might result in challenges, such as students avoiding a task because they are not sure how to use a particular technology. Proactive teaching involves developing individual student relationships and cultivating classroom community so that when academics become difficult, the trust that has been established by strong relationships and open communication can assist students in working through frustration supported by the teacher or even by each other.

Many teachers also equate proactive teaching with avoiding behavioral difficulty during instruction. This is because anticipating student needs prior to where learning connections break down and understanding is inhibited raises student motivation and willingness and reduces frustration. One method schools have relied on to enhance academic, social, and behavioral outcomes is to employ the use of positive behavior supports (Sugai et al., 2000).

The use of positive supports as a process or approach rather than a curriculum, intervention, or practice arose to highlight the relationship between behavior and academic success (Sugai, Horner, & Gresham, 2002). This means that when we are proactive about providing support, we can help students to avoid frustration, embarrassment, or challenging behaviors that interfere academically or socially.

Universal design for learning is one way that teachers can be proactive in considering instruction; the Center for Applied Special Technology (CAST) has developed three guidelines that work well in concert with proactive teaching.

UNIVERSAL DESIGN FOR LEARNING

All teachers know well that each classroom (each year!) is comprised of a community of students who bring their own unique approaches to learning in the door with them. Does the evolving diversity in the classroom actually make the traditional model of instruction more laborious and less efficient for teachers? Expecting all students to benefit from the same methods of instruction can keep classroom instruction stagnant, inadvertently favoring some students and disadvantaging others. Today's classrooms require instructional methods that are as diverse as our students, but simply the sheer desire to do this is not enough.

Universal design for learning is a research-based set of principles for curriculum development, teaching, and learning that accounts for the diversity of learners in the classroom today and emphasizes instruction that aligns with the learning networks of the brain. It's a concept that was originally borrowed from architecture. Architectural design did not always account for use by certain groups of people, such as the elderly and those with physical disabilities. As a result, physical barriers made these public spaces inaccessible. Although accessibility could be improved by adding special features to buildings such as ramps, chair lifts, and elevators, these solutions are expensive, inefficient, and finicky (not to mention unattractive and segregated). This challenged architects to think about how to design spaces that accommodated those who may have specific access needs in the design stage, *prior* to construction. These accommodations can produce benefits for everyone, not just the group for which they were intended.

This concept is easily parlayed into education settings. How can we design instruction *prior* to delivery to account for differences in order to avoid time-consuming, reactive, and separate accommodations/modifications that create potentially isolating conditions for differently abled learners? Using this ideology, the needs of a broad spectrum of learners can be considered from the planning stage of instruction (CAST, 2011; Meyer, Rose, & Gordon, 2014).

Although the UDL guidelines are a comprehensive framework of sorts, they are a foundational concept of the X framework to help educators consider how to utilize technology as a means to both engage and convey knowledge to students more efficiently and variably (representation), as well as to provide students with new opportunities to demonstrate knowledge (action and expression).

CAST, the purveyors of the UDL guidelines, makes it clear that UDL guidelines in and of themselves are not specifically related to technology, but UDL guidelines used in conjunction with XFW are useful in considering how technology can be utilized to improve access to the curriculum. They serve as one quadrant of the X framework for this reason: to provide an essential stanchion for forming the opening to curricular access. The UDL approach involves three principles:

1. The ways we engage students' attention.
2. The methods by which we represent information to students.
3. The opportunities we provide students to demonstrate what they know as the result of their learning.

Using XFW, each of these areas can be enhanced with technology, which we detail further in part II of this book.

To illustrate how technology can enhance the principles of UDL, consider how student engagement could be enhanced with interactive lecture slides that allow students to actively interface with the teacher's content. Information that was previously presented to students in written form only might be read aloud or recorded in advance, supplemented with video, or customized based on various literacy levels. To reflect their understanding, students that previously may have demonstrated learning via a classroom presentation might instead create a podcast, design a website, or craft a series of social media posts. Each of the UDL principles is outlined below in greater detail.

Principle 1: Multiple Means of Engagement

Principle 1 of the UDL framework focuses on student engagement, which begins with an exploration of how to inspire motivation and ignite interest in the student. It calls for teachers to use a variety of strategies and resources to gain and maintain student interest and to promote student organization and self-regulation (CAST, 2011). CAST suggests that engagement is related to the affective network of the brain—or, as they posit—"the why of learning"—and involves how students become engaged, are challenged and interested by the learning, and are motivated to learn (2014).

Have you ever started to introduce content by providing a verbal description, only to observe students' eyes glazing over or students starting to fidget (almost immediately)? Students become engaged in and feel motivated to learn more about academic content differently. For some, interest is sparked because a student may have personal investment in a particular topic; perhaps they pay special attention when learning the parts of a cell because a parent works in a laboratory. Yet others might prefer novel approaches, such as the opportunity to make notes about cell structure using a picture before hearing any background information. A teacher could engage students using technology such as Pixlr, by creating a digital cell while explaining, or by taking students on a field trip to a virtual biology lab.

The critical part of this principle according to CAST is that information "that does not engage learners' cognition is in fact inaccessible" (2014). Engaging the learner is half the battle!

Principle 2: Multiple Means of Representation

Providing multiple means of representation suggests that singular instructional approaches, such as simply lecturing or providing only text or only audio, cannot adequately address students' needs; therefore, teachers should provide multiple options for students to access the content (Meyer, Rose, & Gordon, 2013; CAST, 2011). CAST suggests that representation is related to the recognition network of the brain—"the what of learning"—and involves how students gather facts and categorize academic content that they hear, observe, or read (2014). This principle is about how students understand and register the knowledge that is presented to them.

As teachers know well, students understand information in a range of ways, and much of this is related to their individual learning needs. This suggests that a diverse classroom of students learns best from exposure to a variety of instructional supports that convey the same content. Consider teaching the concept of time to a classroom of students. It would be great if everyone learned it one way, the first time, but that's unrealistic. There may be some students who perceive this content best through traditional explanation, others through the experience of using digital models, a group that learns time through repetition of their own schedule, and yet others who might benefit most from watching digitally elapsed scenes as the sun rises and sets.

Interestingly, though, all of these means can reinforce each individual student's primary means of understanding the content. When instructional materials are flexible, designed with the classroom community of learners in mind, multiple ways of representation help to ensure that all students can benefit. In other words, you may provide options for representation for your students because some of the students need it, but all of your students can benefit from it.

It's useful to interpret this aspect of the UDL guidelines as a focus on creating learning contexts and conditions under which all learners have multiple opportunities to access the learning content. To create such conditions, teachers must provide options for students to perceive, receive, and comprehend the content. Singular instructional approaches may fail to reach the array of learners in the classroom, but when the number of opportunities to access the learning increases, the likelihood for comprehension for an increased number of students is also greater.

Principle 3: Multiple Means for Action and Expression

The final principle of universal design for learning is providing multiple means of action and expression. CAST (Meyer, Rose, & Gordon, 2013; CAST, 2011) offers that this aspect of the guidelines suggests that all learners vary in their navigation of learning environments, including expression of knowledge and the strategy, practice, and organization to do so. CAST suggests that action and expression is related to the strategic network of the brain—"the how of learning"—and involves how students plan and perform academic tasks, especially how their ideas are organized and expressed (2014).

This thinking can be extended to learning contexts and conditions, meaning that the way a learner approaches one aspect of learning, such as math, might be dramatically different from how they approach, for example, literacy. The conditions under which the learning materials are presented to the student may have important consequences for their own approach to learning. This is why providing multiple means of action and expression, as the UDL guidelines suggest, is critical to optimizing learning and deemphasizing factors that we once might have considered obstacles to learning, such as disability, language or cultural differences, or socioeconomic status.

For example, perhaps a class has completed a curricular exploration of the Romantic era and has been asked to prepare a presentation describing one aspect of life during this time period in New England. If all students were assigned a single means of doing this, such as writing a report, it might produce uneven results, whereby some students achieve the expectation and others do not, some students receiving accommodations and others modifications of the assignment. What if instead students were allowed to produce their work using a wide variety of action and expression through the use of technology? This would allow students an opportunity at the outset to achieve the desired outcome without significantly changing the expectation of the assignment.

For example, a student who struggles with writing might instead choose to demonstrate what a rural town in New England looked like by employing Google Maps to zoom in on Old Sturbridge Village, narrating particular aspects of life in a rural New England town. Another student might choose to write the report using speech-to-text software such as Dragon; yet another might use Podbean to record a podcast about music during the Romantic period. Each of these methods allows students to capitalize on their own strengths in approaching the assignment, and all of them provide the students with an equal opportunity to meet the academic expectation.

This principle of the UDL framework can also be incorporated by schools by instituting a concept called genius hour. Genius hour is an approach to learning that empowers students to determine what they learn during a set period of time in school. Usually, students spend a portion of every day or week focusing on a topic of personal interest and are given opportunities to share their work of choice with other students, teachers, and the school community at large. The idea is that when students work on something that is interesting to them, their motivation to learn increases. Genius hour is a powerful way to embrace diverse interests, promote student-centered learning, and engage students in an authentic manner. It is also aligned with UDL in many ways, since students select the learning tools that match their own learning profile, allowing teachers to address a wide range of strengths in a single classroom. In fact, UDL is a necessary foundation for authentic implementation of genius hour. Technology can help to bridge the gap between student passions and authentic learning during genius hour implementation as a logical extension of UDL—it's the difference between personalization to meet *all* needs and personalization to empower student autonomy and personalized learning.

This aspect of the UDL guidelines can be interpreted as a focus on creating the conditions under which learners have the appropriate means to demonstrate or show their knowledge. To create such conditions, teachers must focus on instructional planning and supports that allow students flexibility in learning and academic processes and products that "provide alternative modalities for expression, both to level the playing field among learners, and to allow the learner to appropriately (or easily) express knowledge, ideas and concepts in the learning environment" (Meyer, Rose, & Gordon, 2013; CAST, 2011).

THE X FRAMEWORK SO FAR

Three of the X framework quadrants have been detailed to this point: technology fitness, proactive teaching, and universal design for learning. Technology fitness helps teachers to evaluate their own comfort level for technology use in the classroom and to make decisions about when, what, and how to implement it. Proactive teaching is a simple concept that underpins a complex aspect of teaching, wherein teachers must achieve a healthy balance between planning, in advance, to support student needs in concert with the content and delivery, creating a way to address student learning differences and responding to learners in vivo as they work. Universal design for learning helps teachers to think carefully about the "why," "what," and "how" of learning, enlisting student interest through multiple methods of introducing content across the curriculum, expanding the ways that content is conveyed, and providing opportunities for students to demonstrate their knowledge. Next up is the final quadrant of the X framework, assistive technology, which provides the final element in creating curricular openings for students using technology.

Chapter Four

Assistive Technology

My needs were accommodated through technology in such a way that—despite sometimes crippling communication difficulties—my abilities became the focus.

—Kimberly Gerry Tucker, artist and author

WHY WE NEED TO IMPROVE ACCESS

3,081,240. Three million eighty-one thousand two hundred and forty. That's the number of students in grades K–12 who were suspended from U.S. schools during the 2009–2010 school year according to a report released by the Civil Rights Project at UCLA (Losen & Gillespie, 2012). Why is this important?

According to the report, students with disabilities were more likely to be suspended repeatedly in a given year, which is the opposite experience of students without disabilities. Additionally, students of color with disabilities experienced even higher rates of out-of-school suspensions. This means that students with disabilities are experiencing disparate disciplinary exclusions resulting in lost or decreased instructional time.

Students with emotional, intellectual, multiple, and learning disabilities additionally experience the highest dropout rates (Johnson, Thurlow, & Schuelka, 2012). Additionally, the lowest achieving 25 percent of students are *twenty times* more likely to drop out of school, compared to students in the highest achievement quartile (Carnevale, 2001). Students with disabilities are at greater risk for dropout than peer groups (Thurlow & Johnson, 2011). Across the United States, the rate of graduation for students with disabilities is abysmal, reaching only 63 percent in 2014 (National Center for Education Statistics, 2015).

This means that students with disabilities not only need the supports we have previously described—teachers who practice regular self-evaluation regarding whether their practices match their beliefs, teachers who inventory their own technology fitness, teachers who engage in proactive teaching and use classroom and digital technology—but such students also may need much more to access the curriculum to find their place in the classroom, to stay in school, and to have the same opportunities for success as their typically developing peers.

AN ENTITLEMENT, NOT A PRIVILEGE

An important distinction here: the use of assistive technology for students with disabilities is not merely part of good teaching, good practice, nor is it a privilege—it's an *entitlement.* It is required by law under the Individuals with Disabilities Education Act (IDEA), the nation's most recognizable federal special education law, which protects the rights of students with disabilities who receive services in U.S. schools.

Under IDEA, assistive technology (AT) is defined as "any item, piece of equipment, or product system, whether acquired commercially off the shelf, modified, or customized, that is used to increase, maintain, or improve the functional capabilities of a child with a disability" (Individuals with Disabilities Education Act, sec. 300.5).

AT ensures student success in the general education classroom by providing students with disabilities with the tools and conditions to *access* the curriculum. This is good for teachers, too, because it offers teachers opportunities about how to rethink access to the curriculum for other students in the class—meaning it can be good for other students as well.

This does not mean that students with disabilities who require the use of assistive technology should share them with other students who may benefit—rather, it means that the type of support that is put into place can be good for all students. This is a starting point well aligned with the X framework (XFW). When assistive technologies for students with disabilities are designed to improve access to the curriculum as the result of a learning need on the part of the student, they serve to redress the balance of the classroom.

For example, perhaps a student is distracted by the scraping of chairs across the tile floor and has difficulty focusing as a result. The educational team or teacher designs a solution "to increase, maintain, or improve the functional capabilities" of the student. Let's say the solution is to place tennis balls on the feet of all of the chairs in the classroom to reduce noise so that the learner has fewer distractions to tune out when trying to focus on academic work. When assistive technology has been leveraged to support this particular learner, all students benefit from a quieter environment.

Another example is a student with graphomotor dysfunction, which results in both motor and visual challenges when writing. As writing crosses the curriculum, the student requires the support of assistive technology to access the curriculum, which could take multiple forms. One might be the use of a computer for typing writing assignments, speech-to-text software when required to write on demand in class, or the option to orally record narration rather than writing when the evaluation doesn't include writing as a core component of the academic task.

It's clear how these kinds of supports benefit student with disabilities in accessing the curriculum. The extension of benefits to other students relates back to the XFW. Providing the type of supports detailed above—using a computer for writing assignments, speech-to-text software, or recording narration as options may increase the motivation and interest of the other students, improving participation and offering greater opportunities for them to showcase their knowledge. (Does this sound familiar? It's a direct connection to proactive teaching and universal design for learning.)

With the infusion of technology into our society, these kinds of assistive technology supports are more seamlessly delivered in the classroom than ever before, meaning that such items, programs, tools, or handmade supports are used on an almost daily basis by many K–12 students. For students with disabilities, this means the supports they are entitled to and that they require for access to the curriculum do not result in them being singled out or treated differently in the classroom.

ASSISTIVE TECHNOLOGY USE IN THE CLASSROOM

Although assistive technology use in the United States is difficult to estimate (Carlson, Ehrlich, Berland, & Bailey, 2001), likely in part due to its broad definition under both IDEA and the Assistive Technology Act of 1988, academic research indicates that it results in greater educational opportunities for students with disabilities. This means that assistive technology is *necessary* to access the curriculum, and again, this needs to be differentiated from the use of technology for typical peers.

For example, consider the quote at the beginning of this chapter by Dr. Stephen Hawking, arguably one of the smartest and most highly regarded scientists in the world, who uses an augmentative and alternative communication (AAC) device, which falls within the context of the definition of assistive technology as defined in IDEA. This communication device is in place to assist Dr. Hawking with communication, but his use of it has not affected his ability to achieve—rather, it has been *because* of his device that he could continue writing, researching, and giving speeches.

Students with disabilities may use many assistive technology devices across a school day to access the curriculum, and they may have the most to gain from educational and digital technologies used commonly in daily life, such as smartphones and other personal devices—especially those that can be customized based on individual need and preference. This alignment of common use that results in better access can also alleviate stigma from the use of "special" devices—that is, assistive technology that calls attention to itself while supporting learning (Parette & Scherer, 2004).

One example that illustrates the difference between individual and classroom use is when a student with a disability who requires assistive technology to access the curriculum is the only student provided with it. Again, it's important to emphasize that such supports are very different than simply using digital or educational technology in the classroom. They are an entitlement for students with disabilities who receive special services. However, there's a case to be made for considering how employing XFW can make for improved and more equitable implementation.

Consider a scenario in which a student with a disability is the *only* student to be provided a device to support writing (word processor, laptop, computer) during a writing assignment in the classroom. A remix of this would be where all students were provided the *option* of using a device for their writing assignment. This doesn't change the requirement for the student with a disability and it also doesn't privilege any student over another—it simply expands the means by which students can complete the assignment. Today, with more and more schools adopting 1:1 computing environments, bring-your-own device policies, and using educational technology regularly, assistive and educational technologies are converging. This means that although assistive technology must remain specific to a student, the goals of proactive teaching and universal design can be realized more fully.

In some cases, especially in the past when technology was not so readily accessible for so many K–12 students, stigma could lead to technology abandonment among students who would have otherwise benefited from using it (Hargreaves & Braun, 2012). Given the cultural shift toward more widely embraced and common technology use, it's easy to conclude why using technology may provide excellent opportunities for all students. In the same way that technology can serve as the foundation upon which to create learning environments that are flexible and customizable, assistive technology can provide necessary curricular access for some learners in seamless, non-stigmatizing ways.

WHO USES ASSISTIVE TECHNOLOGY?

Any student with a disability who requires the use of any item to assist with access to the curriculum is a student who uses assistive technology. As the definition dictates, AT items, devices, or supports can be "acquired commercially off the shelf, modified, or customized." Therefore, something as simple as an index card that helps a student to focus their eyes on the lines of text as they read is assistive technology.

Given their unique and specific learning needs, students with disabilities may seem particularly suited for the use of assistive technology. To illustrate this point and extend it to show how AT works within XFW, we examine specific learning disabilities (SLD) as an example. Under IDEA, the term *specific learning disability* means "a disorder in one or more of the basic psychological processes involved in understanding or in using language, spoken or written, which may manifest itself in the imperfect ability to listen, think, speak, read, write, spell, or do mathematical calculations" (IDEA § 300.8 [c] [10]). Learning disabilities occur in approximately 8 percent of all U.S. students and are considered a high incidence disability area (National Academy of Science, 2015).

Students with specific learning disabilities may fail to respond to well-implemented evidence-based instructional practices in one or more core academic areas (Jackson & Karger, 2015). Given this, students with SLD may be particularly well-suited to benefit from assistive technology, as well as the kind of technology recommended for use within the XFW—reflecting, as we noted above, the convergence of assistive and educational/digital technologies.

This is true for a number of reasons. First, modern digital technology serves two primary purposes: to compensate for particular weaknesses and to capitalize on strengths, which matches well with the variation in strengths and limitations in students with SLD (Lewis, 1998). In addition, students with SLD often have academic trouble in one or more discrete areas such as reading written text, writing in a structured format, or employing executive functioning skills (National Association of Special Education Teachers, n.d.). One-to-one technology can now be customized to meet the individual needs of particular students (Lei & Zhao, 2008).

Second, assistive technology that is provided on an individual basis is sometimes seen as providing an unfair advantage on assessments for students with SLD (Edyburn, 2006). This attitude reflects a preference for "naked independence" or performance without external supports or resources (Edyburn, 2005). In classrooms, this bias is at times reflected in teacher resistance to the use of such technology, even for the purpose of skill development, because it disadvantages other students, creates conditions that are not always replicable, and relies on tools that will not be allowed on standardized tests (Edyburn, 2006).

Third, nearly a third of assistive technology devices are abandoned by students with disabilities (Todis, 1996). Reasons for AT abandonment include difficulty of use, perceived value in learning, and challenges faced in repairing damaged equipment (Mull & Sitlington, 2003). In addition, students with disabilities often abandon assistive technology that illustrates an obvious difference with their peers, making one-to-one technology a better option than individual technology in terms of social anxiety (Riemer-Reiss & Wacker, 1999; Hargreaves & Braun, 2012).

In considering how some of the social stigma of use of AT devices for curricular access could be leveled, consider what we know about one-to-one technology. First, it has the potential to increase the self-efficacy of students with specific learning disabilities (Steiner, 2017). One-to-one access also provides an opportunity for students to master the tools associated with a particular device (Penuel, 2006), which may alleviate the academic frustration common among students with learning disabilities (Sawyer, Graham, & Harris, 1992). This is particularly important given that self-efficacy is so closely associated with students' attitudes toward learning and achievement (Zimmermann, 2000).

There are other challenges to one-to-one environments, such as the digital divide referred to in chapter 2. However, the real challenge may lie in the nature of teachers' and students' use of technology, not just in its mere presence (Warschauer et al., 2014), one of the reasons we developed XFW. Extending to assistive technology is important—research cited earlier suggests that technology abandonment is a significant challenge for individuals with disabilities, and this is often the result of poor training or follow-up equipment (Mull & Sitlington, 2003). Improving the confidence, skills, and expertise of teachers with all technology can help to address this.

ORIGINS OF ASSISTIVE TECHNOLOGY

New York Times writer John M. Williams coined the term *assistive technology* in 1982. Williams utilized computer-based speech therapy to assist him with a lifelong stutter. In the process of writing about his experience, he arrived at the term *assistive technology*, and it passed muster with his editor. Before long, the term was generally accepted to describe various forms of technology that support those with disabilities (Family Center on Technology and Disability, 2008).

Over time, definitions of AT have begun to highlight differences between digital assistive technology and traditional digital and educational technologies. Assistive technology represents a particular type or use of digital technologies that mirrors the federal definition and "increase[s], maintain[s], or improve[s] the functional capabilities of an individual with special learning needs" (Edyburn, 2000, p. 127).

Usually, assistive technology is categorized into three or four categories, referred to as the "assistive technology continuum." This might include no/ low tech, mid tech, and high tech. No/low tech usually refers to easy-to-use, free or low cost assistive technologies that typically do not require a power source. For example, these might include highlighters, sticky notes, or reading panes.

"Mid tech" is considered easy to operate, may require a power source, and may require some training for use. Examples might include an MP3 player or a scientific calculator. High tech refers to the most complex programmable technology, which always requires a power source, tends to be more expensive, and requires training for proficiency of use (including for the student, staff, and parent). An example of this might be an AAC device or an electric wheelchair.

ASSISTIVE TECHNOLOGY AND UNIVERSAL DESIGN FOR LEARNING

One powerful bridge from assistive technology to teaching and learning is universal design for learning (UDL), given that the UDL model emphasizes flexibility in order to meet the needs of students with a variety of learning preferences (Rose and Meyer, 2002). UDL requires an examination of curriculum in the ways we engage students' attention, how we represent information to students, and how students demonstrate what they know or can do.

All of these areas can be enhanced with technology. For example, engagement can be enhanced with interactive lecture slides that allow the audience of students to interact directly with the presenter's visual content. Information that was previously only presented to students in written form can be read aloud, supplemented with video, or customized based on the reading level of the student. Students that may have demonstrated learning via a classroom presentation might instead create a podcast, design a website, or craft a series of social media posts.

For some, assistive technology and UDL are complementary or even "two sides of the same coin" (Rose et al., 2005, p. 507). Others question whether UDL is possible without technology (Edyburn, 2010). However, there is no doubt that digital technology can support UDL in ways that were previously impossible (King-Sears, 2009).

A technology-infused UDL school environment will not succeed without broad backing for the use of technology to support learning (Morrison, 2007). However, the challenge of integrating technology in classrooms that are already faced with myriad demands on teacher time is a reality to consider. One way for technology to support the needs of students with disabilities *and* the learning of all is to identify common classroom technologies that can be customized for individual students using the X framework, which supports teachers to think about their own technology fitness and encourages teacher agency in adopting technology aligned with their practice.

IN CONCLUSION: ASSISTIVE TECHNOLOGY AND THE X FRAMEWORK

Assistive technology comprises the final quadrant of the X framework. Although Assistive Technology is required for use by many students with disabilities, the likelihood is that at least one student in every class will use it, given that 84 percent of students with disabilities are in general education settings for the majority of the day. Having put all four quadrants of the XFW together, each with its own unique features and supports offered to students, consider how the opening for curricular access can be formed when all four best practices are put into motion.

Chapter Five

Remixing School Culture with Technology

If you attempt to implement reforms but fail to engage the culture of a school, nothing will change.

—Seymour Sarason

Despite the ubiquity of technological change in nearly every area of daily life, some classrooms appear to be virtually unchanged from those of fifty years ago: desks arranged in rows with the teacher at the front of the classroom; learning materials arranged on the periphery of the room; technology assigned to the corner or a lab down the hall. Tradition is also commonly reflected in the way that learning occurs; the teacher fills the role of "owner of knowledge" and students the "empty containers" waiting to be filled.

There are a number of reasons for this relative stagnation in the evolution of teaching and learning in the face of so much technological change, but most are unrelated to teacher resistance. The reality of school-based technology, unfortunately, is that funding is often inadequate and inconsistent. When there *is* funding for technology, teachers are almost universally not provided adequate time or training to integrate the use of technology in meaningful ways. Finally, school and district leaders may feel reticence in moving forward with a schoolwide technology policy or lack confidence in demonstrating technology leadership. This keeps educational technology as a "sidelight" from the essential work of the classroom and can result in keeping classroom instruction immune from the overall pace of technological change.

Perhaps there's a way to honor what works but improve it at the same time. Think of the musical remix we described in chapter 3—different from its original form but with some of the same elements, along with additions or

41

changes to create a new version. Both are usually appealing—sometimes to different listeners. Remixing the classroom can work in the same way: using the essential elements of the original, remixing it to offer a new version that incorporates its best elements, but adding new features so that it undergoes changes that create new opportunities and experiences for learners that promote access and engagement.

ACCESS AND EASE OF USE

Despite funding constraints, the relative availability of technology has improved so dramatically that it is beginning to make a dent without significant shifts or investments on the part of districts. One reason for this potential shift is that advances in computer hardware and software have made substantial improvements in ease of use and access. In other words, sophisticated technology now comes standard in many of the "basic" technologies. This results in better access at the foundational level of technological investment.

As time has passed, access to the Internet has also improved dramatically. Wireless access is no longer considered a luxury for many government-owned buildings, including schools—even "antique" traditional brick-and-mortar schools in which the original design did not include wireless technology. Many school systems have capitalized on U.S. government programs, including the federal E-Rate program, which provides telecommunications, Internet access, and internal connections such as broadband services at a discounted rate with the purpose of outfitting schools with universal or near-universal wireless access. This has increased support for capital funding requests, not only for the provision of wireless access, but also for its improvement.

DIGITAL DEVICES:
NECESSITY IS THE MOTHER OF INNOVATION

Wireless access has also given schools more flexibility in the types of digital devices and ways that they are used and integrated into classroom instruction. Traditionally, schools have relied on stand-alone computer labs filled with desktop computers tethered to wall outlets with power cords and network cables. This made sense when the role of computers in school was limited to a highly technical platform for teaching challenging scientific concepts, technical design, and computer programming. However, the role of computers has expanded over time to include content area work, to encourage research, to assist with preparation for standardized tests, and more. As classroom teachers invested in the use of computers, access and availability declined if they were housed in a shared, tethered physical space. Before long, technology use in most schools was primarily driven by the computer lab calendar rather than by any learning goals.

The introduction of lower cost, easier-to-use mobile devices that utilize the school's wireless network for connectivity has changed this paradigm completely. Among these devices are iPads, which were first introduced in 2010, Chromebooks, first introduced in 2011, and Microsoft Surface, first introduced in 2012. These mobile devices has allowed schools to invest in portable carts of devices that can be wheeled into a classroom on demand, booted up in seconds, and used without any complicated network setup. In addition, there are a wide variety of applications for these devices that can be managed at the school or district level, easing trepidation about them being unreliable or confusing to use that may accompany new technologies.

A MENU OF CHOICES FOR DIGITAL TRANSFORMATION

Based on the revolution in network access and device flexibility, new models of school technology use are challenging historical patterns of use in which technology was tangential to the everyday business of the classroom and challenging the traditional model of classroom instruction wherein the teacher was the content expert and the students the novices. Among these are the "one-to-one classrooms," bring-your-own-device model, flipped classrooms, and blended learning environments.

One-to-One Computing

One-to-one schools are perhaps the purest model for school technology use. In this system, the school or district provides a common device to every student, which is used during school and often can be used at home as well. One-to-one offers a number of benefits to the successful integration of technology.

First, teachers no longer have to worry that a computer lab won't be available or that a cart of devices will be signed out already. Every student has access to a common device. Second, because every student (and often the teacher) is provided a common device, the comfort level of the teacher and the students is maximized. Less time is spent trying to interpret the functioning of the device, which preserves more for actual learning. Finally, concerns about a potential digital divide at home are alleviated (though not completely).

Access to a personal device ensures that all students have adequate computer time at home as long as a home wireless network is available. Schools can mitigate the challenge of network access for students without wireless by providing a data-enabled mobile phone device, subsidizing the cost of wireless access, and providing extended evening and weekend availability at town and school locations with wireless access.

Classroom Party: Bring Your Own Device

For school systems that are not ready to absorb the financial burden of a one-to-one model, the bring-your-own-device (BYOD) model is an attractive alternative. With BYOD, students are given a rough guideline of acceptable devices and are individually responsible for bringing their devices to school each day. The advantages of BYOD are concrete: the burden of the expense of technology use is transferred from the district to families. This also alleviates the challenge of sustaining an expensive technology program over time. On the other hand, what BYOD gains in affordability, it loses in consistency. Even with guidelines, student devices vary, creating a challenge for teachers who cannot be familiar with every possible device configuration.

Blended Learning

Skepticism about fully digital classrooms has led to a number of compromise or hybrid models of technology integration. Each case includes a limited integration of technology that attempts to produce the benefits of technology integration while maintaining elements of traditional instruction. "Blended learning," one of the more popular hybrids, is a combination of traditional face-to-face instruction and computer-based learning. Several forms of blended learning have been explored, including the rotational model in which students are led by schedule or teacher direction to either online or traditional forms of learning: the flex model, which is primarily online but with face-to-face teacher supervision; self-blend, wherein students select online courses as a component of an otherwise traditional schedule; and the enriched-virtual model, in which all of a school's courses have online and traditional components (Staker & Horn, 2012).

Blended learning has the potential to offer many of the benefits of one-to-one and BYOD models while maintaining a foothold in traditional teaching. Some classrooms have found this a perfect balance while others wrestle with tendencies to view computer-focused time as a diversion from the primary goals of the classroom.

Flipping the Classroom

Another compromise model is the "flipped classroom," (options for which we also detail briefly in chapter 8), which shifts the traditional information transfer component of instruction from the classroom to the Internet and asks students to access the information outside of class time. In-class activities are aimed at clarification, reinforcement, and discussion of the information that students had previously absorbed. A nondigital conception of the flipped classroom has existed for decades in the form of homework designed to serve as the foundation of classroom discussion. Digital technology has allowed the classroom component of the flipped relationship to be more dynamic and engaging. However, a successful flipped classroom asks a great deal of students in terms of self-direction and organization, which may be too much for some students.

Build It (and They Will Come)

Physical school environments are also beginning to reflect changing attitudes in relation to technology. This is partially driven by the makerspace movement, which we detail in chapter 10, a philosophy that calls for individuals to be given the time and tools to experiment in an open and collaborative environment. Some schools are experimenting with makerspaces as a potential outlet for student creative expression that also emphasizes science, technology, engineering, and math (STEM) skills.

A growing comfort with reimagining traditional spaces within the school is also reflected in changing ideas about the nature and role of media centers, the location formerly known as the school library. No longer are media centers defined by row after row of shelving filled with printed texts and a uniform focus on traditional research and reading. Instead, media centers are more frequently being reimagined as centers of exploration where students and faculty alike explore a variety of independent spaces, each with varying media: books, digital resources, physical objects, and collaborative learning spaces.

The Evolving Role of Teachers

Some predicted that computers would supplant teachers, that as digital resources became more popular, the importance of teachers would wane. Recent experience has disproven this prediction. Although students are able to use technology to access information in meaningful ways, teachers have taken on the challenge of curating this vast supply of information and the responsibility for guiding student understanding of what it all means.

One of the benefits of easier-to-use technology is that technology-related professional development has shifted its focus from the technology itself, instead emphasizing the integration of technology.

Teachers are also more frequently developing personal learning networks (PLNs) to inspire effective technology use and to promote ongoing learning and flexibility in pedagogy. PLNs are informal networks of resources, which may consist of e-mail groups, social media platforms such as Facebook and Twitter, blogs, and other digital collections of knowledge. The benefit of a

PLN is that it is entirely teacher driven, designed as such that the locus of professional development shifts from other district or school staff to the teacher. With a PLN, an individual teacher can develop a bank of resources that matches his or her needs or interests and access it on demand. A PLN also doesn't require face-to-face interaction, maximizing productive learning time.

SOCIAL MEDIA IN SCHOOLS: BE THE OWL, NOT THE OSTRICH

Possibly no topic in educational technology invokes as much fear in parents or teachers as social media. This is understandable: research reflects that by middle school, 92 percent of teens age thirteen to eighteen use social media daily (Lenhart, 2015). However, many students may lack the maturity to use it appropriately. Unsafe or risky behavior might take the form of sharing too much personal information online, engaging in or falling victim to cyberbullying, or failing to balance technology use with family time, schoolwork, or most importantly, fresh air.

The answer to this challenge is not for schools to go into a digital lockdown mode, blocking every known site that enables students to communicate with each another and directing teachers to avoid social media like the plague. This strategy is bound to fail for a number of reasons. First, though it does make sense to block access to anonymous chatting platforms like Ask.fm and Chat Roulette, it is impossible to block every social media site out there. For every site that we discover as a school system, developers are out there creating two more, and students are finding them. Second, hindering access to known sites pushes students to find others that are less well-known and more likely to attract unsavory characters. Third, students quickly discover that basic productivity sites such as Google Docs can be used to chat—by sharing a document and working on it at the same time. Basically, blocking "everything" and sticking our heads in the sand won't work.

So, what should schools do about social media? Try the three E's of schools and social media: embrace, educate, and empower.

1. *Embrace* social media as a school resource. Create a school Facebook page, encourage administrators' use of Twitter, share school photos via Instagram. What will this do? It flips the forbidden and mysterious nature of social media to open and public. The hope is if we treat it as no big deal—something boring that even adults do—students will be less likely to use it dangerously because it won't be so enigmatic. They may even be more likely to share their own social media with teachers and administrators, making it part of the regular conversation in their academic spaces.

2. *Educate* students about the benefits and potential pitfalls of social media. Rather than using the duck and cover method, make social media part of the curriculum. Give students opportunities to use social media in a structured and supervised environment and to understand its dangers—and to make mistakes where they can be addressed immediately.

3. *Empower* students to use appropriate collaboration platforms to participate in meaningful discussions with other students. Kids love to chat, to connect online, to express themselves in ways that are only possible in a digital environment. Make online engagement a regular classroom activity and satisfy students' need for interactivity.

The fact is that social media is here to stay and kids are going to use it. Channeling the ostrich and putting our heads in the sand doesn't help anyone. The alternative is to be the owl: find wise uses of social media that guide students in the right direction.

LEADERS WHO WALK THE WALK

In order for schools to drive the wave of change rather than to be the driven, schools need to be guided by effective school administrators and teacher leaders who are able to "walk the walk" with technology by demonstrating an appreciation for technology that is central to their professional practice. It's understandable for school leaders to feel enormous pressure due to factors such as performance on federal and state-mandated tests, many of which distract from a broader vision for classroom technology use. If schools and districts set policies that encourage effective use of technology and promote appropriate experimentation rather than resisting change at every turn, social media can be used as a venue for unpacking assessment results, reaching a variety of families that may not have otherwise connected to school communication, and for an improved community presence.

Part II

Remixing the Classroom

There is always a step small enough from where we are to get us to where we want to be. If we take that small step, there's always another we can take, and eventually a goal thought to be too far to reach becomes achievable.

—Ellen Langer

Chapter Six

Technology As a Classroom Pillar

It is important to remember that educational software, like textbooks, is only one tool in the learning process. Neither can be a substitute for well-trained teachers, leadership, and parental involvement.

—Keith Kruger

STRIKING THE RIGHT BALANCE

In today's age of accountability, wherein critics of education abound and there's a palpable emphasis on standards and test scores, many teachers must rely heavily on instructional materials designed to help students meet standards. Increasingly, classroom teachers have to create instructional materials with the specific purpose of aligning to standards, which often relate to education reform initiatives that can be controversial for educators. Creative, thoughtful teachers now must work increasingly hard to find the spaces to think outside of the box, usually with little to no time for planning or professional development. There are many ways to augment traditional approaches in a student-oriented way that create an accessible curriculum, all while striking the delicate balance between reform mandates and maintaining teacher autonomy over instruction. Technology is a perfect complement to traditional approaches and when utilized responsibly can create spaces for learning where only barriers existed previously. In this way, technology becomes a pillar for the classroom.

Technology can play a critical role in making the curriculum more accessible to students of varying ability levels, but as we've said earlier, it must be done thoughtfully so that the technology is a match to the instruction and the learner. There is widespread concern with regard to the infusion of technology into preK–12 classrooms, particularly as an increasing number of districts are adopting one-to-one technology environments (meaning that the district encourages the full integration of technology in every classroom, with one digital device assigned to every student).

The concern, as we discussed in the previous chapter, is understandable— how will we balance traditional instructional approaches with the digital age? However, ready or not, students are utilizing digital devices. For example, the 2017 national Speak Up survey revealed that 90 percent of ninth through twelfth graders, 77 percent of sixth through eighth graders, 47 percent of third through fifth graders, and a whopping 36 percent of kindergarten through second graders are personal smartphone users. Tablet statistics are on the rise with younger users as well: 60 percent of sixth through eighth grade students, 59 percent of third through fifth grade students, and 52 percent of kindergarten through second grade students use tablets. With these statistics, it is clear that part of the job of the educator is to ensure students use devices in ways that help them to be active, engaged learners who use technology *responsibly.*

Embracing technology and making it an asset to learning helps everyone, including the educator. Technology can be an essential tool for promoting student engagement, and learning and incorporating it into lesson planning improves universal design. As educators responsible for the design of curriculum and the education of tomorrow's citizens, we need to be the guardians of how technology is introduced to ensure that its purpose meets the ideals of public education.

Technology can complement the expertise of the teacher, enhance the curricular decisions made in the classroom, and may be globally beneficial to all students. Since we have outlined how teachers can evaluate their personal readiness for technology use, we next describe foundational supports for the classroom that can help improve accessibility, using tools that may be already within reach right in the classroom.

COMMUNICATION AND COLLABORATION

Get Your Head in the Clouds: Cloud Storage Technology

Although most people are familiar with the term "cloud storage" by now, the concept is still mystifying to others. Cloud storage can be thought of as an online hard drive. In a cloud storage model, your data—documents, presentations, photos, videos, and other materials—are stored remotely rather than directly on your computer. Cloud storage immediately improves storage space and is convenient for teachers who want to organize their digital instructional materials.

When using cloud storage, documents are accessible from anywhere, from any device (computer, phone, tablet, etc.) that has Internet access. The basic idea is that an average computer user ultimately will acquire more data than their computer can manage and will need another place to store it. Cloud storage allows a user to move data off a traditional hard drive onto a remote server, using the Internet to connect to it. Additionally, this content is protected from hard drive crashes and viruses that often destroy information stored on classroom computers, which makes it attractive to school districts that are legally bound to defend district data.

There are many examples of cloud storage services, and many more are becoming readily available for use by districts. This kind of storage solution will "hold" all of your documents, spreadsheets, presentations, videos, photos, and more in one place, making it easy to organize and making it easily accessible to you and to students, if you choose. One of the many benefits is the ability to access your documents from anywhere you have an Internet connection, which also makes collaborating on the documents easy as well, whether with colleagues or with students.

Cloud storage is a solution for students with organizational or executive function challenges—this may conjure an image of the bright but struggling students who have hundreds of papers hanging out of their notebooks, folders, and backpacks. Such students might need guidance about what is useful to keep, what is extraneous, and how it should all be organized. One of the many features of cloud storage is that documents can be organized into digital folders according to specific classes, and within those, folders organized by date, task, or any other way that makes sense to the student.

Folders stored in the cloud and the documents within them can often be worked on collaboratively and synchronously by users in two different physical spaces. Sharing documents and folders digitally is incredibly easy, it can provide a forum for group work and editing, and it offers storage of files and information, which are accessible to the user anywhere there's an Internet connection. This makes it easy for the teacher to check and provide feedback on documents themselves, but also on the organization of them, especially for students who need help mapping their work into a specific plan.

Many cloud storage services such as Google Drive and Microsoft One-Drive offer e-mail to school systems for free, and as a result, many are implementing cloud storage as their primary means of collaborating, sharing documents, and collecting information. Given their ease of use, they offer incredible value for both teachers and students.

Given its popularity within educational settings, we offer examples of features of Google Drive. Many districts have adopted Google Classroom (detailed later this chapter) as a companion to Google Drive. Drive's file-sharing capacity allows document to be given with either view-only rights or editing rights. If a user assigns documents as view-only, invited users such as a teacher or classmate can simply view the document in Drive. This function might be useful for teachers to be able to check the working progress of assignments before feedback is appropriate. If users are assigned editing rights, they are able to contribute to and comment on the document—excellent for group work, feedback, and grading.

Drive also offers a revision history that shows what each user has contributed, and if necessary, the option to restore a particular version. Lost assignments can be a thing of the past with Drive and other cloud storage services that allow document storage and editing. By creating a digital version of assignments, students are then able to customize the content to fit their needs. For example, users can customize text size and color to meet visual needs, take advantage of Drive's built-in screen reader, add captions to video content, or insert comments to document notes to themselves. Drive also converts PDF images of text into editable text (still not a perfect science, but a great tool for handouts that teachers may only have as PDFs and especially good for students who don't handwrite).

Cloud storage is convenient, but it also offers users a way to create a central hub for the classroom. Modeling this practice also encourages students to use it for their own document management. Rather than struggling to remember to bring in homework completed the night before (or struggling to even *find* the homework assignment in a pile of papers!) students can share it with the teacher when it is complete with one click. This also allows students to collaborate on homework assignments without physically being together, as well as to edit each other's work and provide peer feedback. Documents can be edited in real time; some services allow users to see text on the page as it is being written or edited. Cloud storage also saves drafts automatically as students work (thereby completely obliterating the "dog ate my homework" excuse).

Benefits for Teachers

- Manages documents for professional practice and for the classroom in one place
- Creates an easily accessible forum to provide feedback to students
- Allows teachers and students to work on documents simultaneously and authentically
- Allows teachers to "check in" with students without singling them out

Benefits for Students

- Revision history allows for easy editing and tracking of document changes
- Drive is integrated with a growing number of useful add-ons to supplement its functionality, including mind mapping, definitions, and bibliographic information

Examples

- Google Drive
- Microsoft One
- Dropbox

One, Two . . . MP3

An MP3 is a compressed digital audio file intended to retain excellent sound quality while minimizing file size. Most downloadable music, for example, uses the MP3 format. MP3 files can be used for many classroom activities; the best part is that MP3s can be created and shared quickly, easily, and painlessly. MP3 files can be made easily using personal music devices such as iPods, apps, free web tools, almost any cell phone, and most computers. The potential uses for MP3 files are truly endless for both teacher and students. The beauty of this approach is that it is readily available on almost any digital device—computers, phones, and web-based apps—and can instantly improve accessibility.

Consider a busy classroom in which students with different strengths in different curricular areas work at varying levels. Providing directions and repeating the directions as reminders and for clarification are an expected part of teaching. For some students, recalling and/or understanding directions following instruction is laborious and challenging and can be a roadblock to even attempting extension work. That can be remediated by the teacher taking the time to create a quick audio recording of the directions that is available to anyone in the class who may need it. This makes the support invisible for the student who can't work without it but is also helpful for other students who need clarification or a refresher. Other teacher uses might include providing feedback or comments on student work or audio reminders for due dates. Students can record detailed explanations of their thought processes on a particular problem, any questions they may have so they don't forget them, or even a presentation for the class.

There are easy ways to share MP3 files, as they are small and can be e-mailed, posted, or left on inexpensive MP3 players around the classroom. There are also web-based platforms for organizing and sharing podcasts, which are short audio clips designed to be a quick, low bandwidth form of information and entertainment. For teachers, a podcast can be an effective supplement to classroom instruction on any topic and yet another way for students to learn in- and outside of the classroom. For students, a podcast is a resource that can be used on almost any digital device and taken anywhere.

All personal computers and most smartphones are now developed with simple tools for recording content, which can be easily transferred to any web-based hosting service, some of which maintain a database of podcasts created by users. Podcasts are available today on almost any topic, from Italian or Latin language instruction and English grammar to Islamic history or computer coding—and that's merely scratching the surface! Podcasts are an excellent way to help expose transition-age students to their articulated interests and provide an opportunity to explore new interests.

Benefits for Teachers

- Can minimize repeated explanations or instructions by creating short audio files that students can access anytime
- Can create messages for students and/or parents with nuance that e-mail or text alone lacks
- Can be easily created and shared via e-mail or website

Benefits for Students

- Students can access digital files anytime, anywhere
- Students can utilize teacher audio files to review directions, critical information, or static assignments
- Students can easily use this technology themselves—for example, creating an audio file of required homework rather than writing it down

Examples

- Audacity is an open-source web platform for creating and editing sound, enabling a computer to serve as a center for podcast creation. The greatest benefit to Audacity is its ease of use—the download is simple to use, with clearly labeled buttons to guide the user through recording (the interface buttons look like those of a tape recorder!). Audacity even allows a user to create digital files of records or tapes, preserving important content that may be in old formats.
- Podbean is a hosting solution for podcast creators that eases the challenge of managing and monitoring large numbers of audio files, since it is hosted online on the website. Once you have created a podcast using any of the tools mentioned above, your file can be uploaded to the Podbean website quickly, where it is automatically added to a customized, personal site that can be shared with others and/or embedded in a school website. The Podbean platform also provides detailed usage statistics, so that teachers know if their podcasts are being heard by just a few students or the whole school community.

It's All That: Learning Management Systems

Learning management systems (LMS) are exactly what they sound like— software that provides organization for the administration of online educational content.

Learning management systems such as Google Classroom, Moodle, It's Learning, Blackboard, and Edmodo offer a blank slate for a teacher to create a digital community for the classroom. This begins with the creation of class "shells" that serve as the primary mode of organization. Each class is assigned a code that connects enrolled students to their teacher. The shell may also give a teacher access to any participating student in the district, which creates the ability to add students manually (for example, students in another grade or building). Educational content can be created with the additional benefit of the use of embedded content from any other website, and students can work at a teacher-determined pace or at their own leisure if the teacher so determines.

With a learning management system, a dashboard of current "classes" and assigned work appears upon log in. Usually, assignments can be completed right within the LMS and turned in directly to the teacher on the site. As students turn in assignments, they are organized automatically in the teacher's account, with an overview of the class's progress on assignments. Assignments can be reviewed, graded, and returned to the students with comments in the digital interface.

Benefits for Teachers

- Capitalizes on the use of digital technology while honoring the critical elements of traditional instruction
- Enhances and improves existing classroom approaches
- Centralizes content for students

Benefits for Students

- Content is easily accessible
- Approach to enhanced content is via the same process, eliminating or reducing extraneous steps for students

Examples

- Google Classroom represents the technology juggernaut's first foray into the market of learning management systems. Given Google's strong educational presence, there's no doubt that it will be a major player in this crowded field. Google Classroom offers many of the same features as other LMS systems, but when a school system's teachers and students are already using Google as a primary platform, the technical component of the LMS becomes more transparent and less of a burden on teacher and student. Classroom also recently joined forces with Quizlet (discussed later in the book).

• Edmodo
• Blackboard
• Moodle

IMPROVING ATTENTION/REDUCING DISTRACTIONS

I Can See Clearly Now: Web Page Editors

Web page editors essentially clear a web page of any content that's distracting, unappealing, irrelevant, or contains a solicitation that teachers may not want their students to see. Essentially, they are a house cleaner for web pages!

Web page editors allow the reader to transform any web page by removing "clutter" to improve visibility. This addresses a major challenge for students with disabilities related to decoding or visual processing, as the majority of modern web pages utilize multiple sections, including banners and images. This is especially true of news websites used regularly in educational settings. CNN, for example, has three sets of top navigation bars, a lead story with an image, a live video feed, headlines, an album of other top stories, weather, and stock market quotes—without even scrolling down the page!

Most web page editors allow a user to specify visual preferences, including the size and font for displayed text, either black text on a white background or vice versa, and the length of individual lines. Once you open an article and engage the editor, the web page is instantly and cleanly transformed. In addition to the text formatting, the software removes all of the additional material surrounding the text, including secondary navigation bars and images.

When a web cleaner is installed, the browser always has a button for quick access to the program's tools. Options for "clipping" the page range from saving the whole page to selecting the main article to simplifying the interface of the text and removing any clutter on the page. Users can also bookmark the page or take a screenshot. Any of this content is saved to the user's Evernote account where it can be stored, organized, and shared.

Benefits for Teachers

• Removes unappealing, irrelevant content, including ads
• Reduces visual stimuli on web pages
• Reduces web page distractions

Benefits for Students

- Decreases distraction
- Allows students to focus on critical information on the page

Examples

- Mercury Reader (Chrome browser, iPad) offers the features of a standard web page editor and also serves as an integrated bookmarking tool that allows readers to save articles for later viewing and to read recommended articles from others.
- Evernote cleans pages and makes them available for printing cleanly. It also allows users to save articles within the Evernote workspace.

Caption This: Captioned Media

Captioned media is an essential element of learning for students who are visually impaired, blind, deaf, hard of hearing, or deaf-blind. It makes the content immediately accessible by adding text to visual media. It also makes content more accessible to English language learners who may have difficulty following auditory content.

This is a necessary and important technology, and here we feature the Described and Captioned Media Program (DCMP), which is an unparalleled database of augmented media available free to users with vision or hearing disabilities (or teachers of these students). DCMP is the result of a partnership between the U.S. Department of Education and the National Association of the Deaf. Registering for the DCMP website provides access to a searchable database of four thousand educational videos that include descriptions, captions, and transcripts. If you plan to show educational videos in your class, DCMP is an excellent, simple resource to improve accessibility for learners who need visual reinforcement of the auditory content.

Benefits for Teachers

- Reduces prep time for accommodations and modifications of content for students with disabilities
- Assists in reaching a variety of learners in the classroom, including special populations

Benefits for Students

- Improves accessibility, reducing the need for special accommodations since the tool is available to the entire class

• Increases access to complex language, and may boost vocabulary and literacy development

Examples

• Described and Captioned Media Program (DCMP)
• YouTube allows users to caption existing videos. After uploading, users select "Captions" from the Edit menu, and edit as the video plays.

CLASSROOM EQUIPMENT

It's Not Skynet: Computer Accessibility Features

Unbeknownst to many teachers, a wealth of savvy, easy-to-use technology is right at their fingertips. Windows-based PCs, Macintosh, iPads, and Google Chromebooks have a wide range of robust accessibility options that are good alternatives to cutting-edge technology and worth exploring with students. These technologies provide excellent options for representing content in multiple ways and are included in the standard functionality—meaning they are built in and ready for use!

PC (Windows 7)—Windows accessibility options include an adjustable magnifier that enlarges the screen from 100 to 1000 percent and higher, a narrator with a variety of options for voices, rate, and pitch, and a high contrast theme for students with visual impairments. These can be accessed in the "Ease of Access Center" found in the control panel.

Apple (Mac OS)—Apple prides itself on accessibility features, a major focus in the last operating system. All Macintosh computers have an extensive selection of options to customize use of the device, including options for those with vision, hearing, motor, and print text challenges. All Macs are equipped with VoiceOver, a screen reader that utilizes advanced voice technology. Macintosh computers also have robust text-to-speech functionality, called Dictate, which allows users to dictate anything that can be typed.

In addition, users can adjust the size of the cursor and replace an auditory alert with a screen flash to indicate when a program needs the user's attention. Macs even have switch technology built into the operating system. Finally, almost any Mac function can be controlled with voice commands. All of these tools are located in System Preferences, under Accessibility. iPad has the same range of assistive options and also provides a number of options for modifying the use of the touchscreen using AssistiveTouch. This allows users to customize common touchscreen functionality, such as tapping to click and pinching to zoom.

Chromebook—Google's laptop computer, has similar capabilities. Once logged in, users can go to Advanced Settings to change display settings, cursor size, and enable spoken feedback. The Chromebook also supports some Braille displays that allow text to be presented in Braille format.

Benefits for Teachers

- Accessibility features offer many free and embedded tools to support students to access curriculum and increase their independence
- Computers are a common classroom tool, allowing students to access curriculum without stigma, and they can be used as a means for differentiating instruction

Benefits for Students

- Literacy tools allow students to independently preview text by hearing it before being required to read it without audio
- Keyboards and mice can be programmed to meet the individual needs of learners
- Experience can be highly customized to meet learners' needs

The New Chalkboard, 100 Years Later: Interactive Whiteboards

The chalkboard was introduced into the classroom in the late 1800s, and it held on as the backbone of instruction for—brace yourself—*almost one hundred years*. Although the whiteboard was invented in the 1960s, it did not enter the classroom for many years. These days, whiteboards are found more often than chalkboards in classrooms. The whiteboard was not a major change to the functionality of the chalkboard—other than improving readability—until the 1990s, when, like so many other awesome things in this period, the *interactive whiteboard* was born.

An interactive whiteboard allows computer images to be displayed on a board using a digital projector. The images can be manipulated by the teacher or facilitator directly on the screen. Options for this interactive experience continue to grow, providing more flexibility and lower costs as time goes on.

There are three primary forms of interactive screens available. The original whiteboards consist of specialized white boards embedded with cameras or projector/board combos that are synchronized. Another type of interactive display is the interactive projector, which allows the projector to be installed above any regular whiteboard. The projector is paired with one or more digital pens and a classroom computer, which allows the teacher to manipulate any displayed content directly on the board. Because the board is a regular whiteboard, the teacher can still use regular dry-erase markers when needed.

The final platform for display interaction is an interactive system, which is a magnetic bar that sticks to a regular whiteboard and uses a paired digital pen to control onscreen content. This is a significantly less expensive option than the others presented, and it is portable, offering greater flexibility to school systems that regularly have teachers moving from room to room.

The value of these products is immeasurable. This interactive experience versus the traditional "chalkboard" lecture creates an engaging and active foundation for students, and the use of an interactive display allows teachers and students to work collaboratively to manipulate content material, detached from individual computers or the teacher's computer station. Such a platform also provides the ability to manipulate digital objects directly on the screen, which is particularly powerful for students with fine motor challenges who may struggle with clicking and dragging objects on smaller computer screens. Students are able to demonstrate their work and participate without any accessibility issues.

Benefits for Teachers

- An interactive surface allows the teacher to manage the classroom display from the front of the room rather than being tied to a device
- Abstract concepts can be displayed graphically and manipulated directly on the screen

Benefits for Students

- Students can control content directly with the fingertips
- Students tend to be less distracted due to the highly interactive nature of the tool

Examples

- SMART Board
- Promethean
- Mimio

Honey, I Shrunk the Whiteboard: Screencasting

Wouldn't it be amazing to shrink the whiteboard and let students take it home? Yep, it would. Meet *screencasting*, a concept that rocks. This is a whiteboard that teachers can use to record their own voices, narrate a lesson, write questions, notes, or problems on the screen, and record audio to explain what is happening. Screencasting is app based, so it can be shared online for instant access anywhere!

When you launch a screencaster, a blank white canvas appears with a customizable menu of colors and a record button. Recording begins with the push of a button, and while speaking, a user can write notes, attach photographs from iPad, and type text right onto the screen. When finished, sharing recorded lessons via e-mail or cloud storage is easy.

Some screencasting apps offer the added benefit of live streaming of content on an iPad—either to a Mac or PC computer or to other iPads through an Apple TV connection. This allows the teacher to present to the class on a projector and narrate the work while simultaneously recording what they are doing. The recording can then be shared with students via website cloud storage, uploaded to YouTube or potentially e-mailed.

Benefits for Teachers

• Allows the teacher to create simple review lessons that can be shared with students
• Provides storage and organization for teacher-created narrated lessons

Benefits for Students

• Provides on-demand access to review videos created by the student's own teacher
• Makes it easier to find review content that is directly related to the student's needs

Examples

• Screencastify
• Nimbus
• Screencast-o-matic
• Jing

A Picture Is Worth a Thousand Words: Document Camera

A document camera is a relatively simple technology that offers many classroom options. It capitalizes on a video camera that's specifically designed so that any object placed in front of it can be projected onscreen in real time. This is especially effective for those demonstrations with math manipulatives or artistic techniques or woodshop safety that are not nearly as helpful to students in the back of the room. As an added twist, turn that document camera around on the class. Never has class participation been more motivated than when projected for the whole class to see.

There are a growing range of document cameras to match any budget. At the low end, there are $100-or-less options that provide basic functionality and image quality. These are adequate for projecting manipulatives and written work. Higher end document cameras approach and surpass $500. For the extra cost, these devices produce higher quality images, record video of work as it is being produced, and include software that allows the teacher to edit and organize content as it is produced.

Benefits for Teachers

• Makes it easy to ensure that all students have access to materials presented visually
• Some document cameras can record the teaching process for sharing with students

Benefits for Students

• Provides a good view of classroom manipulatives and other teacher/student created materials
• Creates more opportunities for students to showcase work to the entire class

Examples

• Ipevo
• HUE HD
• Elmo
• Avervision

Turn It Up: Soundfield/Classroom Amplification Technology

Sound amplification systems work by projecting the teacher's voice throughout the room so that every student can hear the teacher's words clearly. The teacher uses a microphone on a lanyard worn around his or her neck or clipped to a lapel. Speakers are placed strategically in the room so that the teacher's voice can be heard from every seat. Historically, these systems have been used with students who are deaf or hard of hearing, but in recent years, research has explored how they can benefit a variety of differently abled learners.

This sounds simple, but it can have a major impact. Students with hearing loss are able to access instructions that they may have missed without such a system. Students with attention difficulties find the virtual proximity more engaging. Additionally, the microphone can be shared with students who are presenting to the class or during a fishbowl discussion.

Benefit for Teachers

- Ensures equity in the provision of auditory directions or cues

Benefits for Students

- Avoids the possibility that teacher directions won't be loud enough to hear and understand
- Eliminates concerns regarding proximity of seating

Examples

- Lightspeed Redcat
- Oticon Amigo
- Williams Sound

THE TAKE-HOME MESSAGE

This chapter highlights resources that can help teachers to differentiate the presentation of information to students with a particular focus on multisensory options. Not all of these resources will work for every teacher but keep in mind these general concepts:

- provide layers of technology to represent the content in different ways;
- offer information, whenever possible, to students using multiple senses: visual, auditory, and tactile;
- give students the flexibility to select among multiple options for accessing class information; and
- encourage students to discover digital tools that best serve their needs and to bring them to the classroom.

This chapter highlights resources that can help teachers to lay a foundation of technology in the classroom as the first layer of support. Keep in mind these general concepts:

- You don't have to implement all of these things at once. Try instead to build comfort by starting with one or two.
- Many of the technologies described here can also benefit students at home since they are web based. Recruit parents for help, since they can also access technologies that are web- or cloud-based.

- Many of these technologies are available within items you already use on a daily basis, such as your computer. Take the next step and try to introduce a new tech.

Chapter Seven

Lecture 2.0

In most classrooms, the professor lectures and the students listen and take notes. The professor is the central figure, the "sage on the stage," the one who has the knowledge and transmits that knowledge to the students, who simply memorize the information and later reproduce it on an exam—often without even thinking about it. This model of the teaching-learning process . . . assumes that the student's brain is like an empty container into which the professor pours knowledge.

—Alison King

For years, researchers have concluded that lectures are less effective than a wide range of other educational tools, suggesting that other methods, such as individual reading, are an equally or more effective way of conveying knowledge to students. Yet, despite a growing body of research that suggests that active student engagement can lead to overall positive classroom behavior, improved understanding of concepts, and improved test scores (Freeman, et al., 2014; Armbruster, Patel, Johnson & Weiss, 2009), the traditional lecture—in which the role of the student is largely passive—continues to be the predominant method of teaching in today's classrooms.

What keeps the lecture alive? Here's a look at three key reasons.

1. TRADITION, OR "SAME AS IT EVER WAS"

Lectures have been around since the concept of formal education was conceived, and they have been a pervasive part of the transmission of wisdom and knowledge from teacher ("expert") to student ("novice"). Lectures are as embedded in the tradition of the school day as the schedule, the bell, and the rows of desks. Sir Ken Robinson, a world-renowned education thought leader, consultant, and speaker, once famously noted how education—commensurate to religion and money—"goes deep" with people, particularly their own educational experiences. Education is inherently traditional, and for this reason, it is often perpetuated in the way it has historically been experienced.

2. FEAR, OTHERWISE KNOWN AS "IF IT AIN'T BROKE . . . "

We stay rooted in what we know (or what we think) works. Lecture continues to be a predominant method of instruction at universities, where teachers are traditionally prepared, instilling this method as part of the "craft" of teaching. Today, K–12 teachers are held accountable to reformers' conceptions of "improving education" via an alarming number of new professional responsibilities ranging from content to student evaluation, layered on the natural demands of culturally, linguistically, and educationally diverse students. Increasingly, teachers are being held responsible for student performance that is controversially linked back to their instruction in an evaluative way. Given the deluge of new information, "reform" initiatives, and the data-driven accountability movement, it can be painful to shift our practice to incorporate new strategies.

3. CO$T, OR "THE ETERNAL BOTTOM LINE"

Lectures might not be engaging, creative, glittery, but they are most certainly cost-effective at a time when schools' budget constraints grow and educators' resources shrink. Growing responsibility plus growing accountability minus necessary supports and resources equal less time. To effectively respond to the demands of the classroom, teachers may feel forced to rely on methods that they think will assist in reaching the majority while also managing the precious little time available to prepare.

A TECHNICAL UPGRADE

Here we propose what we refer to as "Lecture 2.0," wherein lecture is transformed into an updated, collaborative, engaging form of teaching and learning in which the educator facilitates the active participation of students while maintaining some of the traditional features or tenets of the original lecture. Lecture 2.0 is a gentle way to ease into using technology in the classroom while ensuring that it is appropriately and ethically matched with instruction as a way to advance learning and not used simply for the dazzle effect.

What follows is a variety of technology tools that enhance and enliven the traditional lecture—even transform it. The effectiveness of a teacher lecture is based on so many factors, including teacher preparedness and expertise, but also on student attention, prior knowledge, interest, and engagement.

Ask Some Questions: Synchronous Polling

One strategy that educators often use to give a lecture a boost is to begin with the pre-lecture, a series of brief activities designed to gauge student knowledge and ignite student interest. Designing this teaching strategy thoughtfully may make a world of difference in the initial introduction of the content, where scaffolding is critical. Pre-lecture activities, such as the tried-and-true "do-now" or icebreaker, can activate student engagement at the start of class, helping educators to connect with students and in turn signal a transition or shift to new learning.

One great way to measure student knowledge or to provoke a discussion before beginning a teacher-led presentation is by simply presenting a question. Synchronous polling software may help to engage students and provide a variety of ways for differently abled learners to respond to the question. Technology forums that support polling are easy-to-use tools for quick poll questions, instantaneous results, and seamless supports for students who might not be willing, interested, or able to participate in class discussions.

There are a variety of polling sites, many of which offer free teacher accounts that allow for 40 responses per poll and an unlimited number of classes. For a fee, K–12 premium accounts offer additional features, such as attendance and grading features, customizable URLs, and printable PDFs of results.

Many sites allow teachers to create an account, and some allow the option of one-time polls. With either option, the process of creating polls and collecting the resulting data is quite simple. First, the teacher selects the type of poll question they wish to ask, such as traditional multiple choice, free response, and true/false questions. Different programs offer extra resources, such as clickable image polls or discourse polls that allow students to give an upvote or downvote to multiple selections. Most free polling resources allow the teacher to customize font, frequency of voting, and type of response.

Students can respond in a variety of ways—by visiting a custom URL (either generated by the site or customized by the teacher), by text, or by visiting a website where the poll has been posted by the teacher. Responses are tabulated synchronously—in real time—and displayed for the teacher to share in the form of a graph, text, word cloud, or clusters.

Longer surveys are also possible. Programs that offer this function allow the teacher to create a set of questions that are shared with students on the Web. As students respond online, results are added in real time to spreadsheets, dynamic charts, and graphs.

Benefits for Teachers

- Provides immediate information about student views, perspectives, prior knowledge, and current performance
- Results can provide a simple, accurate read of student understanding that traditional questioning may not achieve
- Provides a variety of ways for reaching diverse students
- Creating accounts allows teacher to track class data

Benefits for Students

- Provides multiple options for responding to a teacher-led initiative
- Eliminates or reduces anxiety or fear of being called on or of speaking in class
- Provides an anonymous platform for expressing lack of understanding
- Eliminates the requirement of a spoken response for those who prefer not to participate expressively, do not use spoken language, or fear answering incorrectly

Examples

- Poll Everywhere
- Get Polling
- Google Forms
- Stat-Pac

Think Outside the Slide: Multimedia Presentations

For many years, the lecture has been supplemented by multimedia tools designed primarily to supplement a traditional in-person lecture. These multimedia tools, once considered an upgrade to the traditional lecture, can enhance what is being orally presented through use of text and images.

One example is PowerPoint, the longest standing presentation tool on the market, which has been the backbone of multimedia supplemental presentation. It's predictable and simple in form and functionality and was designed to present information in a straightforward and linear fashion through consistent theme and design. However, the trade-off for this predictability is a presentation tool that may fail to encourage innovative thinking and engaging design.

Additionally, this method requires that the lecturer possess effective presentation skills that engage the learner (too often, lecturers are criticized for "PowerPointlessness"—a term coined in 2000 by Dr. Jamie McKenzie). PowerPoint becomes a crutch rather than a tool when riddled with unimaginative slides, pointless dazzle, too much text or when slides are used as oversized notecards that are simply read from rather than used to expand ideas. Although such lectures might organize students' thinking and help them differentiate between important and extraneous content, if misused, the content may be lost on learners.

Lecture 2.0 requires alternatives that emphasize engagement, innovation, and multimedia content, such as nonlinear presentation tools. Such tools allow information to be presented in a three-dimensional space and allow the teacher to navigate in a variety of directions around the central content, including above, below, and to the sides. Nonlinear tools allow fluid navigation during content presentation, enabling the presenter to zoom in and out and to utilize a landscape instead of a slide transition to reveal additional space. This multimedia presentation format is especially effective in illustrating content that is not linear in its organization, such as thematic or cyclical models.

Similar to polling programs, such nonlinear presentation software is available free or at low cost to educators. Users can create an educational account that allows teachers to create, collaborate, and share presentations online and in most cases store content (up to 500 MB in some). Once registered and logged in, the process of creating a presentation is easy, and most tools walk you through with simple directions, illustrations, or audio, making it possible for novice technology users to navigate. Generally, a number of generic templates are available, and all software is different in that they offer distinct features to get you started. Therefore, teachers can choose from an extensive list of content that can be added. Options include adding text in a variety of fonts, colors, and sizes, images, embedded videos, shapes, and diagrams.

Additionally, some linear presentation tools emphasize the use of embedded live content, such as a Twitter stream, blog, or interactive map that update in real time, in addition to other previously mentioned multimedia content, such as audio and video. This allows presentations to come to life as more than static, one-off creations, but instead as live, interactive learning tools that adjust over time.

One example is Haiku Deck, which is both a web-based tool and iPad app for creating and sharing original presentations. The basic version is free but allows only a limited number of presentations to be created. The site emphasizes an easy-to-use interface and presentations with a simple, clean design. Both the website and iPad app are low cost (free to try, with special pricing for educators with qualified education e-mail addresses) and include many presentation themes and millions of background images. Slides can be designed with a photo or solid background, text, or prefab chart including a bar graph or pie chart.

The options presented in this section provide interesting new avenues for delineating content that were created to help boost the appeal of the presentation, improve clarity, and increase access by offering web hosting.

Benefits for Teachers

- Presentations offer a flexible, fluid environment for content in addition to traditional linear tools
- Provides tools for illustrating complex topics including cycles, sequences, and layered content
- Web 2.0 tools can be layered into content, improving engagement and interest and expanding on content
- Most software is cloud based, allowing teachers to access from any computer

Benefits to Students

- Presentations can be made available to students through links, offering opportunities for review and practice
- Use of a variety of media may reach a variety of learning styles
- Improvement on the traditional "one-way" presentations, fostering active learning and engagement
- Features of the software often support Web 2.0 tools already familiar to students

Examples

- Prezi
- Emaze
- Projeqt
- Haiku Deck

Postscript: Slide Libraries

Some of the options detailed earlier also allow the creation of a slide repository for learners to "bank" presentations that can be accessed in the future and by other learners. One example of a slide library is SlideShare, a free presentation and document-sharing repository (a subset of LinkedIn). It's a great tool for making presentations in the format of your choice and available for your students to view online. It's also a vast database of presentations made by others that can be viewed or downloaded for future use. Once registered, any existing presentation or document can be uploaded into the site. Supported formats include PowerPoint, Microsoft Word, and PDF. Each presentation that's uploaded is accessible via a custom URL that can be accessed by anyone with their web browser.

We're in This Together: Collaborative Lecture

A new twist on the traditional lecture involves active, whole class collaboration, which incorporates and responds to student feedback *while* the presentation is happening. This "collaborative lecture" model encourages students to be participants even when the teacher is the facilitator. This method shifts technology from being a potential source of student distraction to a rich foundational tool that serves as the source of engagement. Educators can get a quick sense of student understanding while providing students the opportunity to use technology ethically and aligned with content in ways that break up a teacher-directed activity.

Cloud-based Tools

Cloud-based presentation tools are designed to be an upgrade to linear tools like PowerPoint, allowing much more classroom flexibility. Cloud-based storage relies on the Internet to store all documents online, which are therefore accessible from any computer with an Internet connection. This allows educators to access their work from any computer or web-accessible device rather than saving it to a hard drive or thumb drive. This helps diminish worry about losing work due to computer crashes, provides great organization, and allows more flexibility while preparing.

Many cloud-based tools offer the same "suite" as the traditional tools, including presentation tools, but also word processing and spreadsheets. However, cloud-based tools add more value by offering embedded features. These tools allow a teacher to start with presentation software and add in "layers" of technology, increasing student participation and active engagement.

Since cloud-based tools are similar to traditional tools in many respects, they are familiar to educators and therefore easy to use. Additionally, they offer organizational features previously unavailable with traditional tools, such as activities that are designed to assess individual students, including quizzes, "ticket-out" activities, and team quiz games that allow multiple students to compete on teams against one another. The results of any of these activities can be exported to a spreadsheet that can be saved. Students can view collaborative presentations on their own devices, allowing access at home using websites or apps.

Many of these platforms offer collaborative lecture tools, such as built-in polls, live question-and-answer pages, and quizzes. However, several offer synchronous drawing options, which may excite students inclined toward art or provide access for students with poor handwriting or fine motor skills with alternate response options. Live drawing options include a blank canvas on which students create their own drawings that are immediately available to the teacher. Voilà!—instant feedback and quick, formative assessments can be achieved in a variety of ways that essentially produce the same student data.

Each platform has distinct features, but usually students enter a classroom personal identification number (PIN), which takes them directly to the presentation, though they log in through their own account (which can often be linked with a Google account if they have one). Once logged in, students move at their own pace unless the teacher has chosen to "share" a slide. Once shared, the student account follows along with the teacher's presentation. Embedded quizzes are graded instantly, and students can view individual question results while the teacher examines aggregate scores.

Cloud-based, collaborative lectures are an excellent example of how technology can be used to counteract its own potential for distraction. For the progressive educator or district, they allow personal digital devices to be utilized meaningfully rather than for non-instructional activity.

Benefits for Teachers

- Enables teachers to prepare presentations and notes that can be shared digitally
- Presentations can be created, edited, and presented anywhere
- Quick manner of formative assessment allows teachers to gauge whether students grasp the content
- Allows the teacher to encourage the use of technology in the classroom with less fear that it will be a distraction
- Easy organization of student data for later reference

Benefits for Students

- Allows students to access teacher-created materials at any time or place for review
- Provides a fluid system for students to offer comments or ask questions during the presentation of content
- Provides a variety of alternative opportunities for active participation
- Promotes student attention
- Shifts the presentation platform to the student, which increases interactivity

Examples

- Google Slides is a cloud-based presentation tool with a linear design not unlike PowerPoint. However, because it is web based, it saves automatically, utilizes cloud storage, and allows the teacher the freedom to invite students to contribute comments or content directly to slides. Thus, teachers may accept student feedback while presenting directly on related content.
- Socrative is a student-response system that allows educators to interact with students in their classrooms quickly, to gauge their understanding, and to start a discussion around student responses. With Socrative, students can engage in a poll, take a quiz, complete an exit ticket, and connect to instructional content through their own digital devices. Once registered, Socrative provides the educator a classroom number, which students enter on their own devices. At any point, the educator may select "multiple choice," "true/false," or "short answer question," and students will be cued to respond to the question the teacher has given. Results are tabulated in real time and displayed on the teacher's device.
- Nearpod is an amazing tool for students of all ability levels, but it can be especially powerful for students with disabilities related to organization or attention. Nearpod allows the educator to create an interactive presentation in which students can follow along on their own devices. It includes a variety of assessment tools that provide immediate feedback to both student and teacher. Nearpod has a bank of free and paid lessons created by other teachers and content providers that are also worth checking out.

Speak Up! Student Response Systems

Have you ever asked a question to your class during a lecture, only to hear complete silence? Students are not always eager to speak up in class for one reason or another. Student response systems are wireless and allow students to respond to a question by utilizing a device (also known as a clicker) to select an answer. Student response systems allow students to respond and participate easily and can reduce performance anxiety, such as fear of speaking in front of the class, of giving the wrong answer, or of taking a risk in front of their peers.

Student response systems are frequently employed as tools within collaborative lecture software platforms but can also stand alone. A number of systems consist of a set of devices specifically designed for classroom use with accompanying teacher software that collects and displays responses. These are single-purpose systems, designed to be easier to use than software and more enduring than web-based polling tools.

Benefits for Teachers

- Provides a system for immediate student feedback that can be incorporated into lessons in real time
- Students' investment and collaboration fosters more interest, participation, and less distraction

Benefits to Students

- Permits students to provide synchronous feedback with an easy to use device
- Reduces performance anxiety

Examples

- Smart Response PE
- Qwizdom
- Turning Point

Everything but the Kitchen Sink: Academic Repositories

Academic repositories, or repositories of open educational resources (ROER), are hosts (digital platforms) for open educational resources (OER), academic materials that can be accessed to enhance or extend knowledge or practice on a particular topic. These are large collections of academic materials ranging from video lectures, online courses, content tutorials, and more—all open to browse and use in classroom and home settings. Many sites are nonprofit (some are for profit but still permit teachers access) and offer free registration for preK–12+ educational settings. Registration allows users to save and organize content into playlists for future use. This is especially helpful for teachers who wish to extend their students' learning by encouraging or requiring them to access additional content outside of the lecture, at home, or for further practice.

The theory behind academic repositories is access. ROERs are intended to be an open resource for access to educational materials, in part to improve access to education worldwide. Educational materials posted on the sites are generally from academic or educational institutions, but it's important to know the source of origin when considering use.

The type of content varies on the sites but most cover standard academic content for preK–12+ classrooms, and many align to standards such as the Common Core Standards. Additionally, there are many open college courses that offer great resources and experiences for transition age students.

Benefits for Teachers

• Offers extension materials that may enhance the curriculum
• Multimedia content appeals to learners

Benefits for Students

• Students can benefit from additional explanation or an explanation that utilizes a different approach

Examples

• Sophia helps students to achieve college success. To this end it offers online college courses at a reduced rate. However, it also provides free resources for teachers, including coursework, test prep for students, and professional development opportunities.
• HippoCampus is a vast collection of instructional videos and simulations that can be arranged into playlists and then saved and shared with others. Subjects included in the site's library range from algebra and geometry, physics, biology, and earth science to social studies and English.
• Academic Earth focuses on the global exchange of ideas as the premise for its collection of free academic resources, which are primarily from colleges and universities and range in topic from obesity to war to literature.
• 60 Second Lectures is an initiative of the University of Pennsylvania School of Arts & Sciences. This is a cache of one-minute lectures on topics ranging from poetry to genetically modified foods to Chopin's "Minute Waltz."

Turn It on Its Head: Flipping the Lecture

One popular model of transforming the classroom using technology is "flipping the classroom." This is a pedagogical model in which the information-transfer component of classroom instruction is shifted from the classroom to home. Simply, the typical classroom elements are reversed: lecture at home, homework in class. Rather than gathering information from a teacher or lecture in class, students watch instructor-provided, video-based lectures at home. In this model, classroom time that typically would have been devoted to listening and taking notes is repurposed for active work. This might entail completing enrichment activities and review of especially challenging concepts in groups, through discussion, or by coaching from the instructor.

There's no specific way to flip a classroom or specific tools you need to do it, but one element of the model—recording, storing, and making the lectures available—is a critical aspect. There are free video resources available to teachers, such as the academic repositories mentioned previously, but in this model, it is more common for teachers to create the lectures themselves.

To this end, there are a number of options for recording and storing lectures for future use. Some recording options are free or easily accessible; some are quite expensive. The more expensive the tool, the easier the process of recording and posting lectures. However, it's important to note that "flipping" started with a simple recording tool that worked with PowerPoint lectures, so being creative and using any and all available resources is critical.

Given the technological saturation our society has experienced in the past five years (even in the past five minutes!), it might be easy to assume that most students have access to the Internet at home for viewing lectures, but for those who don't, there are creative ways to ensure access for students. Jon Bergmann and Aaron Sams, the two teachers who first conceived the flipped classroom, suggest that proactive teaching is absolutely necessary to ensure that you reach all students in the classroom (2012).

Benefits for Teachers

- Allows teachers to present a lecture once and record it for future use in a variety of formats
- Teachers can create a vast collection of personal digital resources that can be shared with students

Benefits for Students

- Broadens access to teacher lectures, which can be reviewed at a time, place, and pace that is most appropriate for students' needs
- Creates a resource for students who miss a lecture due to absence or illness
- Allows for deeper engagement with content, as well as with teacher and peers

Examples[1]

- GarageBand (Apple)
- Internal or external microphone (PC)
- Present.me is a presentation tool that merges both a video and slides in a split-screen format, a great option for making lectures available to students online. It offers a free teacher account that includes three recordings each month. Once registered, the process begins by uploading an existing

presentation. Supported formats include PowerPoint, PDF, and Google Slides.
- Panopto for Education (offers a free trial)
- Tegrity (offers a free demo)

THE TAKE-HOME MESSAGE

This chapter highlights resources that can help you to rethink the primary method of instruction for students and amp up student interest. Keep in mind these general concepts:

- Making even small changes to your practice will improve accessibility. It's never a good idea to make dramatic, sweeping changes, since they are difficult to sustain. Slow and steady wins the race.
- Match your technology choices or upgrades to your learners. Technology is wonderful, but it shouldn't be used primarily to make things "sparkle." When used correctly, aligned to specific learner needs, and closely matched with the curriculum, technology is a powerful tool that can be potentially game changing for students.
- Try before you fly: these tools offer different options for achieving your goals. To see the difference, try using an existing presentation to copy content into a new option in order to minimize the work on your first attempt.

NOTE

1. Some of these examples are costly, but remember, simpler versions of this methodology can be achieved by using basic tools!

Chapter Eight

Innovations

To live a creative life, we must lose our fear of being wrong.
—Joseph Chilton Pearce

Traditional brick-and-mortar schools have been criticized by education re-formers for standing still in the face of major technological innovation: cars that drive by themselves, computers that learn by reinforcement (the real Skynet!), and phones that recognize your face. This criticism fails to take into account the incredible social innovations that have happened in schools—the racial desegregation of students, the inclusion of students with disabilities, the coordination of in-school and community support for home-less and unaccompanied youth, advancing protections for LGBTQ students, responding to the increasing number of students who have experienced trau-ma, reducing the consequences of poverty such as hunger and illness—schools are doing pretty well, actually.

The financial constraints of publicly funded schools also have been a consideration for why schools haven't emerged as dazzling products of inno-vation, but even if school budgets weren't constrained, consider that schools may have moved slowly in this regard by choice. Educators should and do look before they leap—in this case, to answer important questions about technology before investing in it. How does a specific technology benefit the learner? How does it align with the overarching goals of teaching and learn-ing? What kind of development can this technology promote? Who devel-oped it and for what purpose?

This careful and thoughtful evaluation ensures that technology that is embraced by and employed in schools has a clear purpose and is aligned well with the goals of education. When it happens, it's magical. Below, two emerging technological innovations that have earned their places in schools are outlined: maker and gaming education.

PART I: MAKE SPACE FOR STUDENT CREATIVITY

In the era of high stakes testing and accountability, student learning can be directed in ways that focus on specific skill development—technical skills that focus more on compliance and repetition than on exploration. This is especially true for younger students, for whom repetitive skill practice can take the place of open-ended activities that emphasize play, tinkering, and creativity. Play has been deemed critical to brain development for the cognitive, physical, social, and emotional well-being of youth, and it allows the development of imagination as well as physical, emotional, and cognitive strengths (Ginsburg, 2007). But increasingly, students as young as early elementary school spend a greater proportion of time practicing a finite set of technical skills based on a prescribed curriculum that's designed to prepare students for the next assessment rather than learning that emphasizes problem-solving skills—activities or learning opportunities that present a problem and the materials with which to solve it.

In answer to the restrictive nature of schooling in the era of accountability, many schools are adopting makerspaces to give students the freedom and autonomy that the scheduled school day and stringent curriculum often lack. Makerspaces take a number of forms, but in general, a makerspace is a place, either geographic or chronological, where students are given the resources to explore and to create without the constraints of direct supervision or assessment. This is a generic term because there's such flexibility in the implementation of the broad idea: give students the opportunity in terms of time, space, and materials to explore and learn in a self-directed fashion. Maker education moves learning from consumption to creation (Bowler, 2014).

Some schools begin the "maker" conversation by identifying a fixed location such as a school library or media center. Others explore mobile solutions in which the makerspace comes to the student. Some create scheduled blocks of time for students to experience the makerspace. Others rely on self-direction during unscheduled time. There is no one correct makerspace model; an important first step is for teachers and school leaders to examine a number of key considerations prior to investing in the "stuff" of the makerspace.

CREATORS, NOT CONSUMERS

Makerspaces can inspire students' confidence in the ability to *create* knowledge rather than only to *consume* it. The maker movement offers support for the idea that the student perspective has value in itself and provides a platform for sharing that perspective. In other words, the ability of a makerspace to inspire confidence in student creation promotes an innovator's mind-set, which emphasizes individuals' abilities to develop answers to complex problems.

When in a makerspace, students engage in creative exploration and problem solving—sometimes with and sometimes without a purpose. Making might involve student experimentation with sound to create musical instruments, building with Legos or K'nex, creating with cardboard, using tools like saws or drills—the sky's the limit. There's only one rule to makerspaces—that things are made there! The *process* is highlighted in this kind of learning—exploring, inventing, tinkering, solving, creating, discovering.

Some makerspace implementations find ways to merge digital and traditional means of student creation, such that students are able to use digital technology to organize their thinking, engage in the design process, and then produce a tangible finished product that can be taken home. This is reminiscent of the approach to learning taken by career education programs (sometimes referred to as "vocational" programs), such as culinary and industrial arts and woodshop. This is a foundation on which maker learning is built—focusing on a creation, experiment, and design and producing a tangible result. It doesn't have to be perfect—the result could be simply what is discovered in the process.

How do traditional skills merge with twenty-first-century skills in order to make them more relevant? Students might use computer-aided drafting software to plan out a project before beginning actual construction; combine elements of robotics with traditional craft supplies like glue and glitter; or build cookbooks with digital tablets. This type of tinkering promotes independent problem solving in a truly unique way (Bevan, Gutwill, Petrich, & Wilkinson, 2015).

One benefit of rapid technology changes is that advanced technologies become readily available to those with limited means. For example, school-friendly "making" or production equipment is now more common and features price tags within the reach of many schools. Lower cost 3D printers, laser engravers, and vinyl cutters, for example, allow students to use digital tools to create designs that can then be produced. This empowers students to engage in a design, prototype, and modify process, which transforms learning from students consuming information and skills prepackaged by curriculum and teachers into students actively learning by creating.

MEDIA CENTER 2.0

As more content is available online and mobile digital devices become more prevalent, schools, school libraries, and media centers have risen to the occasion to remain relevant and current. Student research increasingly utilizes online resources; many journals have moved to online cataloging; and the popularity of e-books have led to many media centers rethinking their primary mission. In order to reimagine—or remix!—media centers as relevant educational spaces, many school and university libraries are embracing the makerspace as a model for twenty-first-century learning.

Makerspaces are designed to encourage students to use a variety of materials and tools to create digital or physical products. In some cases, the emphasis is on traditional artistic media that can be independently used by students to creatively tackle a problem or to invent a story. There are many makerspace materials that are entirely nondigital. In fact, any objects that allow for flexible assembly can contribute to makerspace. This can include Legos, popsicle sticks, and foam blocks, along with glue, tape, construction paper, magic markers, and so forth.

On the other hand, media centers also can be centers of digital creation that encourage student independence. Mobile technology and apps are designed so that students at a wide range of ages can create digital media. Among the common digital tools employed by media centers are green screens and camcorders, tablet computers to be used for photo and video editing, and interactive screens that allow students to collaborate. The hope is that by arranging equipment clearly and providing written guidance on demand, these creator studios can be largely student driven and empower students to work without teachers or librarians "at the elbow." The products created by students might include movies, public service announcements, and persuasive reports that can be shared with the school community.

With both traditional and digital media, media spaces can be places where students explore a passion and find ways to share this passion with the larger community.

It's in the Bag

Makerspaces are versatile. A makerspace does not need to occupy a fixed space (like the media center descriptions earlier) or require whole-class or independent opportunities for students. The makerspace model can also be implemented in a "centers"-oriented classroom by providing a set of challenges that groups of students can take on and then rotate through each center.

One makerspace option that promotes the centers model is the "maker in the bag" program in which teachers create several sets of materials and lessons to bring back to the classroom or use in a dedicated space. This also promotes the use of a variety of media, both digital and offline, within one makerspace.

Benefits for Teachers

- Creates the makerspace directly within the learning environment
- Allows for implementation of the X framework, especially the principles of universal design for learning

Benefits for Students

- No waiting until a specified day, time, or "special" to engage in self-directed learning and tinkering
- Allows students to employ both traditional and innovative representation of knowledge

Robotics

Another aspect of makerspaces that helps to bridge the gap between digital and physical learning tools employs robotics—the science and technology behind the design production and application of student-constructed robots. Robot kits require students to assemble parts with some flexibility and then to program the robot to perform functions. Many of the robot kits emphasize scalability. Younger students with less experience with robotics start with a few components and a simple design. As students become more comfortable with additional components, their creations become more sophisticated, allowing students to remain engaged.

Many kits also include sensors that allow the device to recognize color, distance to obstacles, and light. These interactive components mean that students can develop conditional responsive programming, an essential component of modern computer coding.

Benefits for Teachers

- Allows for teachers to enact the role of "guide on the side" rather than "sage on the stage"
- Telepresence! Teachers can be represented by the robot through a remote connection. This allows you, via Bluetooth, to teach through the robot. Cool!

Benefits for Students

- Exposure to content learning, such as math and science, in engaging ways
- Development of coding skills

Examples

- Lego Mindstorms
- Littlebits
- Makeblock

If You Can Think It, You Can Print It

The emergence of low-cost desktop 3-D printers has allowed many schools to begin integrating 3-D printing into technology. One technique employed in 3-D printing is fused deposition modeling (FDM). FDM is a type of "additive" modeling in which a 3-D model is created by adding layers of material.

Cloud-based platforms such as Tinkercad make 3-D printing accessible by providing a free development platform with a scalable level of difficulty. Elementary to high school students can use such a program, with sophistication of projects increasing as students mature. For example, students design buildings in order to calculate the volume of a solid shape. The buildings are then 3-D printed so the class can collaboratively construct a city. Students may later study more intricate architecture of a time period or culture and design a building representing the period, such as a Greek temple, Islamic mosque, or Egyptian obelisk.

For example, curriculum that exposes students to Italian architecture in an exploration of the Pantheon, the largest unreinforced dome in the world, is an excellent example of how social studies can cross into science. The Pantheon construction required physics to balance gravity and force, something that could be experimented with through a 3-D model.

Benefits for Teachers

- Helps to reinforce abstract concepts with a tangible object
- Allows for teaching across the curriculum (i.e., building a model of the Roman Pantheon)

Benefits for Students

- Promotes student engagement by producing a product that students can take home
- Empowers students by giving them the power to take creative ideas into production

Examples

- Tinkercad (software)
- FlashForge
- Micro 3D
- Printrbot Play
- daVinci Jr.
- MakerBot

Minimalist Computers

One of the downsides of the latest mobile technology, including smartphones and tablets, is that many young people experience computing in a neat little package without the hands-on elements of the early days of the personal computer. In fact, many students reach middle school not having much knowledge of what actually makes a computer tick.

A valuable antidote to this antiseptic technology experience is the user-constructed computer, build-at-home (or school) kits that provide the necessary components to construct working computers, referred to as "minimalist computers." These options vary in their level of complexity and the sophistication needed in the construction process, meaning there are good options for students of all ages.

Minimalist computers provide experiences for the student that enhance already innovative technology, such as taking *Minecraft* interactive, creating a magic mirror that offers daily reminders, or even creating personalized game controllers.

Benefits for Teachers

- Introduces fundamental technical literacy in an authentic manner

Benefits for Students

- Provides hands-on experience with basic technology
- Helps to develop transferrable skills with electronics and computer design

Examples

- Kano
- Makey Makey
- Raspberry Pi
- LittleBits
- Lightup

MADE WITH PURPOSE

So, with all this flexibility, what are the qualities of a great makerspace? Fleming (2015) describes seven attributes of makerspaces that make the difference between an incidental variation in the school day and a truly empowering student experience. Great makerspaces should be:

1. *Personalized.* There is no one-size-fits-all option for makerspaces in individual schools. It is essential that schools design their own maker-space environment based on learning goals and unique elements of school culture. Makerspaces that celebrate local culture are much more likely to make a splash in terms of community engagement.
2. *Deep.* Makerspaces require more than arbitrary elements of creation. Students should find options that build on one another, so that if a student enjoys a basic makerspace option such as building a bridge using popsicle sticks, he or she can take on more advanced engineering and construction challenges. This also helps to align makerspace-developed skills with a standard progression of technological literacy skills.
3. *Empowering.* Makerspaces should allow students to take the lead and use any available resources with minimal teacher support. Therefore, there should be enough guidance so that students know what processes are necessary to use the various materials and options. Unlike many classroom activities, a well-designed makerspace will create a framework for students to guide their own experience.
4. *Equitable.* The makerspace should provide options that fit a variety of student strengths and challenges as described in the X framework. Options for documentation, suggested projects, and potential avenues to share student work can help to ensure that the makerspace serves all students.
5. *Differentiated.* In addition to a selection of choices for resources and activities, students need options for levels of difficulty that can be explored independently. It is essential to provide a set of leveled choices within each set of resources so that students can find an appropriate challenge on their own.
6. *Intentional.* A makerspace without a purpose will not succeed. Building it is not enough to attract students to it or, more importantly, to retain their interest and entice them to return. It's also not enough to develop the kind of teacher buy-in that will make the makerspace sustainable. Teachers and school leadership should design maker-spaces with a specific set of learning goals in mind and consistently describe these goals when describing the space with teachers.

7. *Inspiring*. Part of the job of a school makerspace is to hook students into the joy of creating to learn rather than relying on teacher-led instruction. This requires that the makerspace be sold for its potential: for students to be able to think creatively, direct their own learning, and create something that has the potential to offer improvement and innovation.

PART II: ARE YOU GAME?

Another nascent domain of alternatives to traditional education is the use of gamification to bring authenticity and real-world relevance to the classroom. The use of digital gaming is not a new approach. In fact, video games have been touted as an educational elixir for decades, taking over the mantle of educational disruptor from films, televisions, VCRs, and personal computers. However, there just might be hope for a real impact from video games based on improved access to technology and an improved understanding of what makes video games so irresistible to kids (and adults).

The problem with past incarnations of educational video games was two-fold. First, educational video games were generally developed independently from existing gaming and tended to be poor imitations of real games that favored content over engagement. The price of the emphasis on curriculum alignment was tedium and oversimplification. Second, there was a real problem with how educational games were normally used.

Because these games relied on stand-alone computers and workstations that tended to be in short supply, teachers were left to offer gaming as an occasional reward for students who had completed their regular work or as a few moments' diversion from a regular class period spent in the school computer lab. In such cases, technology was used as an alternative or supplement to the real learning activities of the classroom. Students developed a view of technology and learning that worked in opposition to one another rather than in partnership.

Certainly games present a challenge for the true integration of technology into the curriculum in ways that other forms of technology do not. For example, it's much more obvious how technology can improve a teacher presentation, a reading assignment, or even support student creation of content. But unless gaming is centered as a learning opportunity and not simply a reward or a diversion, it will not produce a significant improvement in student learning.

Nonetheless, nearly everyone between the ages of thirty and fifty remembers *Oregon Trail*, the ubiquitous and beloved adventure game that placed the students' characters in 1848 America on a journey from Missouri to Oregon. In the process of hunting, crossing rivers, and fighting disease, students would gain some understanding of the challenges facing the settlers of the era. *Oregon Trail* has been a hugely successful game with over sixty-five million copies sold. However, it was such a simple model of game play that too little was asked of students in terms of critical thinking, and it only offered a shallow understanding of the dangers of cross-country travel in the nineteenth century.

After three decades of similar games emphasizing simplicity over challenge and content over engagement, the nature of video game use in the classroom is transforming. Specifically, there's an understanding that many entertainment-oriented video games have intrinsic educational value in their need for critical thinking and emphasis on risk taking and that there is value in games with sophisticated game play that asks more of students. The video game industry is also seeing promise in adjusting existing games to add educational value rather than developing educational games that consider entertainment as an afterthought. The end result is a range of games from those that emphasize content with an engaging platform and others that embrace a degree of freedom from curricular coordination and focus more on critical thinking and problem solving.

Understandably, many teachers feel anxious with the concept of gaming in the classroom. There is a sense that students playing educational games is a symptom of a poorly managed classroom or that the teacher is allowing the students too much latitude. In some cases, school administrators reinforce these beliefs. Schools can be leaders in technology and innovation by recalibrating their attitude toward gaming and seeing what it really offers: truly unique potential to engage students and increase learning.

Most importantly, mobile technology is putting games at arm's reach for students in the regular classroom, meaning that gaming can be incorporated more regularly and uniformly. Gaming is no panacea, but it can be a valuable complement to instruction.

There are five broad categories of classroom gaming options: review games, classroom game play, digital simulations, coding platforms, and virtual reality.

Individual Review Games

Though some aspects of traditional review games (games that help students to review previously taught content) have remained unchanged, game makers have learned from the success of entertainment-oriented smartphone games such as *Candy Crush* and *Fruit Ninja*. Although these games are repetitive, they manage to engage users with powerful design sensibilities, special effects, a balance of short- and long-term goals, and a social thread that allows players to track progress against friends.

Many review games have benefited from these lessons and base their own platforms on these games. Though individual review games are primarily created for single students, some allow students to compete against one another and against the clock. Others are very simple re-creations of classic review tools such as flashcards and practice quizzes.

Benefits for Teachers

- Supports review of key content in an engaging format that maximizes student engagement
- Alleviates the burden of developing unique review games for students who need remediation

Benefits for Students

- Empowers students to review independently at a pace and using a format that best matches their learning styles
- Capitalizes on high levels of student engagement with gaming

Examples

- *DragonBox*
- *FunBrain*
- *Knowledge Adventure*
- *BrainPop*
- *Quizlet*
- *EdPuzzle*
- *BrainRush*

Classroom Game Play

Jeopardy!-inspired games have been a whole-class review staple in classrooms for decades. These games inspired student engagement with competition, a flavor of authenticity, and a framework for keeping score that kept things competitive until the end of the class period. These games tended to require significant teacher prep work in recording questions, designing a game board, managing game play, and keeping score. The payoff was a fully engaged classroom that was reviewing key facts and concepts without even knowing it.

The good news is that technological resources have alleviated much of the teacher burden in the new models. The digitized game platforms maximize whole-class interest by capitalizing on mobile technology. For example, some new review technologies allow students to vote or answer using a cell phone, a mobile device, or a laptop. Class performance is calculated in real time and the drama of competition is enhanced with sound effects and background music.

Benefits for Teachers

- Creates an exciting gaming environment without requiring teacher time for extensive customization
- Capitalizes on student access to mobile technology to make these devices an asset to student engagement rather than a barrier

Benefits for Students

- Allows in-class review to be exciting and engaging as well as educational
- Promotes strategies for engaging self-guided learning

Examples

- *Kahoot*
- *JeopardyLabs*
- *Plickers*
- *Exit Ticket*

Digital Simulations

Perhaps the greatest improvement in video games has occurred with digital simulations or online environments that replicate a time period, place, or conceptual framework. Some are constructions with loose ties to reality and empower students as the creators of virtual worlds. Others are less focused on conceptual frameworks and engaging graphics and more on re-creating real-world problems.

Benefits for Teachers

- Provides a structure for student creation while maximizing flexibility
- Provides a safe online environment that empowers students

Benefits for Students

- Utilizes familiar gaming platforms, including *Minecraft*, that are popular outside of school
- Promotes spatial reasoning skills with applicability to a range of subject areas

Examples

- *Minecraft*
- *3rd World Farmer*
- *Get the Math*
- *iCivics*
- *Truss Me!*
- *Kerbal Space Program*

Coding Platforms

A final category of game-inspired technology is the programming platform, which has exploded in popularity along with the argument that computer coding should be considered a necessary skill acquired by the time students graduate high school. Coding is what makes websites, apps, and software work, and coding platforms are now designed for students from early elementary school through high school. This allows students to move from relatively simple graphic-oriented coding to more sophisticated and authentic real-world programming options without extensive teacher guidance.

Examples of student coding projects include playing digital cause-and-effect games, creating an animated video, or telling a digital story.

Benefits for Teachers

- Alleviates the challenge of gaining enough programming experience to lead student learning directly

Benefits for Students

- Provides real-world experience with computer programming
- Promotes student-directed creation by providing a problem-solving platform

Examples

- Scratch
- Scratch Jr.
- Hour of Code
- Tynker
- Gamestar Mechanic

Augmented and Virtual Reality

The latest cutting-edge technology to hit classrooms is augmented and virtual reality (AVR), sometimes simply virtual reality (VR), a broad term that describes any sort of device worn over the eyes that delivers multimedia content directly to the visual field of the wearer. This means that a student is not viewing an experience but is *inside* the experience, interacting in 3-D, with sound, via a head-mounted display. In some cases, the devices are high tech and tethered to a computer; in others, a low-cost headset coupled with a smartphone or digital device serves as the "monitor" for the user via the use of apps.

Content for VR devices is still emerging, but there are a few options worth considering. Google Expeditions is a collection of virtual field trips organized by subject area. Each comes with a series of immersive images and an associated script of descriptions and guiding questions. Teachers are able to use the Expeditions app to direct students to view specific areas of the images with guiding arrows that appear in the students' field of vision. You-Tube has a growing collection of 360-degree videos, including some that explore historical sites, works of art, and geographic features. Finally, a number of apps developed by museums are now available. These apps typically include audio narration as the student "walks" through the collection.

Benefits for Teachers

- Capitalizes on a cutting-edge technology to maximize student engagement
- Uses a multisensory experience to make digital learning more authentic
- Allows the teacher to capitalize on places, experiences, and ideas previously unavailable except in text

Benefits for Students

- Turns abstract concepts and faraway places into more tangible experiences
- Provides exposure and opportunity to learn authentically about diverse cultures, people, and places

Examples

- Google Cardboard
- Oculus Rift
- Samsung Gear VR
- HTC Vive
- Nearpod VR

THE TAKE-HOME MESSAGE

This chapter highlights resources that are innovations in technology and can support increased and sustained student attention, but also allow educators to carve space for creativity and problem solving. Keep in mind these general concepts:

- "Learning by doing" is a research-proven and effective way for students to learn. Don't get hung up on whether "making" and "gaming" seem like "learning." They are!
- Making and gaming cross the curriculum in an engaging way, offering students exposure to math, science, art, design, and literacy in one fell swoop.
- Making and gaming are both student centered and student driven. These kinds of learning opportunities increase motivation.
- Don't take our word for it! Project Tomorrow (2016) suggests that more than 50 percent of students are interested in gaming as a way to learn in school.

Chapter Nine

Show What You Know

*But what if technology took teaching in another direction, with risk-taking—
and a touch of subversion—at its center? Good teaching is not about playing it
safe. It's about getting kids to ask questions, argue a point, confront failure
and try again.*

—Greg Toppo

For some students, perhaps nothing inspires more nightmares than answering
questions in class or presenting to an audience of their peers. Teachers can
likely relate—parent nights, presentations to districtwide faculty, and even
personal commitments such as wedding speeches and gratitude narratives.
Now imagine that same stress magnified by the greatest motivator of student
behavior known to educators: *fear of embarrassment*! Add in other complex
elements of learning such as anxiety, organizational issues, disability, and/or
motivation, and you may have enduring challenges to classroom civics—
participation, group work, peer interaction, and learner investment.

Technology can help to alleviate the obstacles that students may face in
demonstrating their knowledge in the classroom in multiple ways. There are
a range of incredibly innovative tools that, when used creatively, can allow a
variety of learners to access multiple platforms for showcasing their knowledge. These are excellent options for many reasons, the very first being that it
allows students choices for demonstrating how they have learned, and as
discussed in chapter 3, choice can lead to an increase in authentic engagement.

The technologies described in this chapter are further examples of how
technology can help teachers proactively support students, serve the purposes
of universal design for learning, decide where assistive technology is necessary in supporting students with disabilities, and ultimately create the neces-

sary opening for curricular access that is required for some students but that can benefit many.

There are almost endless options for supporting students to demonstrate what and how they have learned with varying levels of technology. Below, you will find a variety of options for supporting students in this way. The best way to model that digital technology is an acceptable way to showcase understanding is to *model* technology for students. Digital presentation tools can help to organize information so that the ideas of the presentation can be both internalized (for the learner) and externalized (for the teacher and peers).

There are also a number of online resources that can supplement traditional presentation with multimedia that can support the learner in engaging the audience. Digital media is available to achieve the expected outcome of a presentation for learners who are shy or not ready for "live" presentation, allowing the learner to record the information in advance but still fulfill the academic expectations.

Last, we can't simply expect that students have the skills to use particular technologies or to know what is expected of them for a particular learning task or assignment. Just as content needs to be taught, the important elements of showcasing knowledge need to be taught as well. Technology is a wonderful support and can help organize, synthesize, and boost student engagement to help students convey their knowledge, but it still requires support and instruction.

However, when students are provided this short-term support, it allows them to dually showcase their strengths and continue to work on their needs with more autonomy once they have been provided brief support. Students who develop confidence using technology also are more motivated to take risks and "tinker" when they encounter new technologies.

GETTING THOSE DUCKS IN A ROW: ORGANIZATIONAL TOOLS

The key to an effective presentation of knowledge? Preparation, of course! We can't expect that all students naturally have the skills to showcase their knowledge in a narrative way. It is critically important to provide students with resources and tools to support them organizationally, which can help to improve clarity. This way, their presentation can showcase, without question, what they have learned and how they enact their knowledge to show understanding.

It's important to support students in understanding that effective presentation is largely about preparation. This includes knowing how to choose an interesting topic, identifying appropriate resources, outlining the information that is gathered, and creating supporting materials including multimedia presentation tools. Without all of this important preparation and legwork, student presentations may fall short of showcasing their understanding of the content.

In addition, a well-organized presentation not only helps the audience to understand the topic, but it also promotes confidence in the presenter. This is particularly important for students who, for a variety of reasons, already may be feeling particularly self-conscious about delivering content to an audience of peers, whether in a small or large group, while being evaluated. There are a number of resources that can guide students in preparation for conveying information to showcase knowledge.

Word Clouds

One type of online technology makes it easy to develop a set of keywords from a document and website based on the frequency that words appear. This technology produces a graphic representation of ideas that arrange words from a digital resource in a shape or cloud by adjusting the size of each word based on the frequency that the word appears, otherwise known as a "word cloud."

This is an excellent way for a student to think carefully about and develop a sense of the most important ideas related to a topic, which can be a challenging task for students. Identifying relevant information and isolating it is a skill required of students of all ages, becoming exponentially more important as students move up through academic grades and reach high school.

Many of the options for creating word clouds were designed specifically for students and thus have a simple interface for generating a world cloud. To begin, a teacher or student either pastes in a text selection or a website address. For example, a student could paste the text from an online encyclopedia or digital reading to help determine main ideas. Two other word cloud generators, Jason Davies's Word Cloud Generator and Tagul, offer the user more power to customize the word cloud based on color and font size and even to arrange text in a shape.

The examples below enable a student to think about the central meaning or key concepts of a topic or reading, an important skill in and of itself, but also one essential step in showcasing knowledge and developing effective presentations.

Benefits for Teachers

* Enables teachers to present main ideas in an engaging, graphic format
* Enables teachers to determine whether a student can identify or repeat the main ideas of a text

Benefits for Students

- Generates a helpful representation of important concepts with just a few clicks
- Empowers the student to independently generate a summary of important ideas
- Gives the student a quick platform for confirming understanding of the major concepts of a text
- Provides a unique visual that can be used in a student presentation or to support a student in conveying understanding

Examples

- Abcya Word Cloud
- Wordle
- Tagxedo
- Jason Davies's Word Cloud Generator
- Worditout
- Tagul

Map It Out

Even more important than identifying the main ideas of content is identifying and evaluating the relationships between these elements. This might include descriptions of the causes and effects of historical events, cycles of scientific processes, and categories that arrange factors based on common attributes. Understanding these relationships is key to conveying understanding, especially in a presentation.

Graphic representations of concepts, or "mind maps," help to make information cohesive as it is relayed, benefitting both the student and the teacher (not to mention an audience of peers). Mind mapping helps students to examine relationships with content by graphically representing the concepts with a series of shapes that are interconnected by lines signifying the relationship between them.

Benefits for Teachers

- Allows the student to focus on understanding concepts rather than the challenge of formatting a graphic representation
- Helps the teacher gauge whether the student can make connections between the concepts and explain why they are related

Benefits for Students

- Offers a simplified platform for explaining difficult to understand ideas
- Creates a visual to which the student can refer when conveying knowledge

Examples

- Text 2 Mindmap
- Bubble.us
- Inspiration
- Mindmeister
- Lucidchart

Bibliography Generators

One essential component of research curriculum, which is required in the Common Core Standards as early as third grade, is the importance of recognizing and documenting sources used in the process of research. Fundamental to this is not only understanding the importance of crediting sources, but also recognizing that thorough research requires multiple sources that represent a variety of backgrounds and perspectives. Teaching students to honor the ideas of others and to provide a record of bibliographic citations helps them to develop a lifelong skill that can be used beyond school.

If you wish to support students in developing bibliographic citations, the downside is, of course, organizing and formatting bibliographic entries, which can be quite tedious, time consuming, and technical, depending on the format. A number of online tools can help students in developing this awareness while also easing the burden of producing accurate lists of citations.

Students begin either by searching for a book, website, journal article, etcetera or by manually typing key bibliographic information such as the author, title, and publisher. In turn, the technology, usually a website, generates a citation that can be added to a bibliography.

Benefits for Teachers

- Reduces the burden of training students to produce highly technical bibliographic citations
- Allows the teacher to maintain high expectations for student accuracy in citations
- Puts the focus on effective writing that cites sources appropriately rather than on the formatting of individual citations

Benefits for Students

- Reduces the time and energy required to produce a bibliography
- Lessens student anxiety about the complex formatting requirements for bibliographies

Examples

- Bibme
- Easybib
- Citation Machine
- Citethisforme

Ready, Set, Engage: Multimedia Supplements

There's nothing more disruptive to a presenter than observing the signs of a disengaged audience: stifled yawns, heads down, glances at a clock. Think of the times you have tried to engage students and have been met with these cues! Now imagine you are a student lacking the confidence to convey knowledge orally or to a group of peers. For self-conscious students, this can be disastrous and reinforce their worries. And when a presenter's confidence wavers, the audience becomes further disengaged, and the presenter may waver further, creating a terrible cycle.

To support students in preparing their presentations, there are a number of kid friendly tools that make it easier to engage an audience. All of these options are engaging, recruit interest (in the words of CAST, 2014), and offer customization, which is an upgrade to the traditional PowerPoint model of presentation. We detailed some of these in chapter 7 when discussing how to upgrade the traditional lecture.

In some cases, such as with Prezi, the technology offers flexibility to explore a topic in three dimensions rather than in a simple linear fashion. This encourages students to think about the topic in terms of layers of meaning, cycles of activity, or progressions over time. Other choices, including Glogster, focus on flexibility within two-dimensional spaces, such as digital posters. Unlike a traditional student poster, digital posters allow for easy embedding of multimedia content, including images and video. In addition, the free-form arrangement of a digital poster allows the student to present with flexibility by calling on resources in a certain order or by giving the audience the opportunity to explore independently.

Benefits for Teachers

- Capitalizes on the flexibility of multiple presentation choices to maximize student engagement

Benefits for Students

- Makes it easier for the student to produce engaging, exciting multimedia as an addition to a traditional presentation
- Offers more flexibility in choices related to the organization and presentation of information

Examples

- Glogster
- Prezi
- Museum Box
- Google Slides

Animation Nation: Tools for Comics and Animation

For many students, animation is a creative outlet, a source of inspiration and empathy, and just plain fun. There are a number of platforms that support student creation of animated images and videos. Animated scenes, presentations, and videos also can be a helpful antidote to the overuse of text that sometimes goes hand in hand with traditional presentation tools such as PowerPoint.

Given the sheer volume of text information that can come with learning new content, asking students to demonstrate learning using other media can be a more productive gauge of how well they have identified the main points. With cartoons, students must present concepts graphically first and with text as only a supplement. This encourages critical thinking and organization of information in a way that text-based tools cannot.

Several animation platforms, including ToonDoo, BitStrips, and Make-BeliefsComix, provide a framework for creating traditional still animations, including single-panel and three-panel cartoons. Presenting knowledge in this format offers a number of benefits for student learning. It requires that students work hard to narrow key information to a particular focus and to develop strategies for illustrating that focus.

Other animation systems provide students with a framework for the presentation of content in video format. For example, iMotion is an easy to use stop-motion animation app. Stop-motion animation, made most famous by Claymation works such as *Rudolph the Red-nosed Reindeer* and *Wallace and*

Gromit, is a unique animation system for creating the illusion of movement. In the past, stop-motion animation required the tedious and time-consuming use of a still camera and the merging of thousands of individual frames. Apps such as iMotionHD and PicPac make this chore much easier by capitalizing on the built-in camera in tablet computers and their large, clear screens. Developing stop-motion animation is still an intricate and demanding process, but these apps ease the process and give the student more time to focus on constructing meaning with the animation and less on technical requirements.

Benefits for Teachers

• Capitalizes on the flexibility of multiple presentation choices to maximize student engagement

Benefits for Students

• Makes it easier for students to produce engaging, exciting multimedia as an addition to a traditional presentation
• Offers more flexibility in choices related to the organization and presentation of information

Examples

• Toondoo
• Makebeliefscomix
• iMotionHD
• StopMotionStudio
• PicPac

Screencasting for Students, Too

For some students, giving an in-class presentation or conveying knowledge orally may take far more effort than is equitable. However, this doesn't mean there's not an alternative that could help the student to achieve many of the goals of an assignment that requires oral presentation. We talked previously in chapter 6 about screencasting for teachers, but this technology is very appealing to students. This technology is friendly enough that students can use and manipulate to create their own videos in the same way, a great alternative to the traditional student group project or presentation.

With digital technology, we can just pack up the whiteboard and let students take it home with them! This concept can support students in practicing or developing the skills for a live presentation or any academic requirement to convey knowledge orally. The technology allows the student to draw, write questions, notes, math problems—anything you can think of—on the screen, and record audio to explain what is happening. Screencasting can be shared online for instant access for other students as well.

These are alternatives that can be fun and engaging for the entire class, especially if the ultimate goal of the assignment is to ensure that the student can convey some command of the subject matter (rather than the ability to give a live presentation, which sometimes is part of the evaluation). In either scenario, completing a presentation using multimedia tools can boost student confidence, help them to develop nonsynchronous oral presentation skills that can be refined and practiced, and showcase their strengths such as creativity or animation or demonstrate the skill, concept, or content being demonstrated.

Benefits for Teachers

• Allows teachers to model live presenation and archive instruction in way that students can access at a later time
• Creates more opportunities to help students meet requirements if unable to present orally

Benefits for Students

• Engaging and fun alternative that improves opportunities for student participation
• Offers opportunities to improve and develop specific skills in a "live" practice format

Examples

• Explain Everything
• Educreations
• Jing

Podcast Away!

Podcasting is an excellent way to inspire students to record content in their own voice, from their own perspective. Podcasts are short audio or video clips designed to be a quick, low bandwidth form of information and entertainment. For teachers, a podcast can be an effective supplement to classroom instruction and an easy way for students to learn outside of the classroom walls.

For students, a podcast is a resource that can be used on an iPod or other portable device and taken anywhere. Podcast files can be posted to a teacher or student website, uploaded to iTunes, or otherwise shared so that they can be played on individual devices such as iPods. For many students, an authentic audience makes all the difference in engagement and motivation. There are many online tools that make podcasting easy and accessible.

Some platforms use MP3 files to improve student learning by creating a web platform for organizing and sharing podcasts—the teacher or student essentially creates a website where podcasts can be stored and organized. The audio files are recorded on a device and then uploaded to the Podbean website. Since all personal computers and most smartphones now offer easy tools for recording content, they can be easily transferred in this way. Podcasting websites also create libraries that include topics such as French and German language instruction, English history, and Islamic history, among many others.

Audacity is an open-source web platform for creating and editing sound, enabling your computer to serve as a center for podcast creation. The greatest benefit to Audacity is its ease of use—the download is simple to use, with clearly labeled buttons to guide the user through recording (the interface buttons look like those of a tape recorder). Audacity even allows users to create digital files of records or tapes, preserving important content that may be in old formats.

There are also websites that require only the press of a button to begin recording podcasts, the ultimate in simple audio recording with a single button interface. Simply click to record, and click again to stop. Once the teacher or student is satisfied with the recording, the file is saved and the recording is provided.

Benefits for Teachers

- Minimize repeated explanations by creating short audio files that students can access anytime
- Create messages for students or parents with the nuance that e-mail or text lacks
- Easily create and share via e-mail or website

Benefits for Students

- Digital files are accessible anytime, anywhere to students
- Students can utilize teacher audio files to review directions, critical information, or for static assignments
- Students can easily use this technology themselves; for example, creating an audio file of required homework rather than writing it down

Examples

- Podbean
- Audacity
- Vocaroo
- iTunes

Augmenting the Textbook

Digital texts (or e-texts, which are digitized alternatives to printed texts) make traditional content more accessible and improve access to the curriculum. The Individuals with Disabilities Act (IDEA) (2004) requires the use of accessible instructional materials (AIM) through the National Instructional Materials Accessibility Standard (NIMAS), which requires publishers to provide digital formats of textbooks for students with print disabilities. Digital texts come in a variety of formats and can immediately increase accessibility by removing challenges that some students experience with printed text. In addition, many are free or low cost, can be updated with new information and editions much more quickly, and provide seamless and immediate access for students at school, home, or anywhere they choose.

Given the specificity of this section and their availability, given that they are primarily federally funded, we provide specific examples and descriptions below.

Benefits for Teachers

- Provides multiple text formats for students to choose from
- Removes barriers for students with disabilities and reduces time spent modifying the curriculum
- Alleviates time-consuming scanning/conversion of traditional readings for students who require digital versions of books

Benefits for Students

- Removing barriers allows students to be immediately successful with the content instead of laboring over the challenges of simply accessing it
- Digital formats allow students to experience the text in a multisensory format by hearing and seeing it at the same time, improving comprehension
- Allows students to access material from home in the same way they do at school

Examples

- NIMAC is a federally funded online file repository in NIMAS format. Promulgated under IDEA, it was established to support authorized users to access more than 46,000 K–12 files that can then be converted to accessible content for students with disabilities. For more information, visit http://www.nimac.us.
- Bookshare (PC, Mac) is an amazing resource that offers a huge database of books (257,000, as of May 2014) available as text, enlarged text, Braille, and text to speech for free to qualifying students, who have physical, visual, learning, or reading disabilities. The Bookshare database includes textbooks, bestsellers, classics, recent releases, and more.

    In order to offer Bookshare services to students, school districts must first complete a contract guaranteeing that they will provide access only to students with documented reading disabilities. Since Bookshare is available through a copyright exception, strict usage guidelines exist in order to honor copyright agreements with publishers. Once Bookshare has received a contract from the district, students can be registered. Required information includes the student's name, date of birth, IEP or 504, and category of reading disability: visual, learning, or physical. Once a student is registered, he or she is ready to start reading books—it's that easy.

    Bookshare also offers free text-to-speech software that can be installed on either a PC or a Mac. Students can have free, at-home access using the same software they use at school so that they can take their work with them (apps for iPad, iPod touch, or Android are also available and discussed later). Using Bookshare provides students who struggle with print text immediate access to literacy, and, as a result, reading can become enjoyable for students overnight.

    For more information, go to www.bookshare.org.

    Louis Plus Database of Accessible Materials, named in honor of Louis Braille, is maintained by the American Printing House for the Blind and offers a database of accessible print materials produced by approximately 160 organizations in the United States. It can help to locate materials in both NIMAC and Bookshare. For more information, visit http:// louis.aph.org/pages/about.aspx.

Text-to-Speech Technology

Text-to-speech technology can organize content from a variety of sources, including websites, compressing it into one manageable, organized, practical digital package that can be used easily by students. It allows for a variety of individual uses by students. For example, in classrooms with several iPads or in districts with one-to-one digital environments, some students could benefit from this technology by using it as a simple e-reader, while another student might use headphones to listen to the text audibly. Since many of these devices are ubiquitous, they make it easier for students who need them for access to use in the classroom.

Students who could benefit from assistive technology could be concerned about stigma from using a technology support that sets them apart from their peers, but the speech-to-text technology of today is available on virtually every digital device, making it easy to use without drawing any attention to students individually. It's also a great way to help any student organize digital content easily.

Two examples are provided here. The first is VoiceDream. When the app is launched, it takes the user to the file library, which at first contains only a welcome message and help documentation. Once there, readers can make adjustments or changes to the augmentative voices. The app utilizes the default iPad voices but offers a number of additional voices for purchase. Each voice also can be customized for speech rate, pitch, and volume.

To add items to the library, first connect to any supporting app—Google Drive, Dropbox, Evernote, Bookshare, and so forth. Then simply tap the "+" (the "add" button) to view any documents or books in that account. Any individual file can be added to the library and will be stored there indefinitely unless removed.

When a document is opened, active words are highlighted as the audio plays. Particular spaces within a document can be also be bookmarked, and the user can fast forward to those places or to any other location in the document. Documents can even be edited directly from the VoiceDream window.

Benefits for Teachers

• Reduces technical challenges associated with downloading virtual texts
• Provides options for students to access curriculum without significant prep work

Benefits for Students

• Reduces stigma in the classroom
• Organizes content from multiple sources (Bookshare, Google Drive, Dropbox, etc.) in one place
• Allows students to manage their use of text to speech independently

The second example is Read and Write for Google, an extension for the Chrome browser, which can be used on Windows or Macintosh computers. There's a free version that includes text to speech and simple text translation.

Once installed, Chrome adds a button to the web address toolbar. When you click the Read and Write button in the browser, you can generate audio for any selected text or translate individual words into Spanish with text and audio on any web page. Or you can use "hover speech" that activates text to speech simply by hovering over a particular word.

The premium version of the software, which was recently offered to teachers for free, comes with a host of features that are built into the Chrome browser and can be used with Google Drive documents. The premium features include text highlighting, regular dictionary, picture dictionary, and word predictor, in addition to the features described earlier. The dictionary allows users to highlight any word and immediately displays a pop-up definition; the picture dictionary displays simplified images that connect with the word. Word predictor is an especially useful feature for students with writing difficulty. While typing in a Google document, the software recommends words.

The highlighter function is especially powerful. All highlighted words and phrases can be sent to a new blank Google Doc with the click of a button. There's also a very useful automated vocabulary builder. Highlighted words are sent to a new Google doc with a text definition and a picture definition. All of these functions can also be used with PDF or uPub documents uploaded to Google Drive.

Benefits for Teachers

- Makes web content accessible to students in text to speech format without additional software
- Integration with the Chrome browser means that any computer can support this application, including Windows-based and Mac OS systems.

Benefits for Students

- Enables text to speech on any computer using the Chrome browser, giving students more flexibility regarding when and where they use it
- Includes a variety of tools for taking notes and organizing information, which allows students to manage their own notes in the same location as the text itself
- Glossary allows for quick organization and formatting of definitions

THE TAKE-HOME MESSAGE

This chapter highlights resources that can help to recruit student interest with technology tools that support their learning, that support their ability to convey their knowledge in the classroom, and that provide opportunities for active participation and removal of barriers. Keep in mind these general concepts:

* Modeling technology use for students helps to improve their motivation to use technology and take risks.
* Support student participation by offering technologies that support the goals of academic tasks but that also provide opportunities for students to work on areas in which improvement is ultimately needed.
* Remember that students still need support and even explicit instruction to use these tools effectively. However, teaching these skills provides great benefits for long-term academic goals.

Chapter Ten

Repurposing Practice

Anything in existence, having somehow come about, is continually interpreted
anew, requisitioned anew, transformed and redirected to a new purpose.
—Friedrich Nietzsche

What exactly is "repurposing"? The concept of repurposing invites transformation rather than replacement. This is a borrowed term, often used in assistive technology, and usually referring to when an item with a specific purpose is reoriented for a different use. In this case, consider repurposing as a
way to shift your practice in a slightly different direction to increase curricular access for all of your students.

Repurposing acknowledges that something has merit and a purpose unto
itself, but also that slight shifts can allow for rethinking, alternate use, or
redistribution of effect. One of the realities of teaching is that the group of
learners changes from year to year. As a result, teachers must also shift and
change to deliver content in a way that is accessible to students.

Repurposing practice suggests that teachers can, do, and should rely on
their own expertise to determine what pedagogical shifts are appropriate,
what level of discomfort (if any) they are willing to experience, and how and
when such shifts in practice should occur.

Historically, the purpose of public school has been closely aligned with
the ideals of democracy, "and yet these beliefs are at risk in schools today"
(Westheimer, 2008). The shift from a democratic focus to one that increasingly emphasizes "preparation for global competition" as a priority education
outcome has created tension for teachers in classrooms across the nation
(Cochran-Smith et al., in press). Teachers feel these pressures in different
ways—consider for a moment how the field of education and the "bigger
picture" influence the classroom—your classroom.

For example, state and federal policy reforms can result in changes at the cellular level of education—schools and classrooms. Although the federal reforms resulting from No Child Left Behind was intended to improve education across the nation, it ultimately ramped up testing requirements in the name of accountability.

Given the consequences of this federal policy, which penalized schools that did not show improvement under its regulations, many educators reallocated instructional time in favor of test preparation, especially since the requirements unfairly disadvantaged some student groups, such as students with disabilities, economically disadvantaged students, and language, ethnic, and racial minorities. Anecdotally, teachers reported feeling fed up, experiencing burnout and lowered morale, and some were even driven from the profession.

Educators are generally actively involved in their schools and the local conversations about education, largely because this context is directly connected to student needs and therefore demands their time and attention. However, it's critically important to understand how larger contexts—policy reforms, critics of education, and shifting priorities regarding the purpose of education—directly contribute to what is expected of teachers and what happens in classrooms.

THE "FAILING SCHOOLS" NARRATIVE

The "failing schools" narrative is not new, but it has helped propel growing public concerns that our schools are in need of improvement, and as the rhetoric has gained steam, blame has extended to teachers (Cochran-Smith et al., 2017). This emphasis on school and teacher failure is often used to justify the array of criticisms and to prompt new policies (Carnoy & Rothstein, 2013) that ultimately affect teachers but that usually do not involve them.

Here's evidence: a 2015 quality of work life survey of educators revealed that nearly 80 percent of respondents did not feel as if they were treated with respect by elected officials (American Federation of Teachers & Badass Teachers Association, 2015), who, of course, are ultimately responsible for creating education policy. Among the many important findings of this survey, one in particular stands out: the major source of stress in the workplace was cited as "the adoption of new initiatives without the proper training or professional development" (p. 4), nicely summing up the mountain of responsibility dumped on teachers by education reforms. Yet these reforms ignore a "fundamental principle . . . policies and practices that are based on the distrust of teachers and disrespect for them will fail" (Tierney, 2013).

What does this have to do with technology? Quite a bit, especially if you are a teacher who is unsure about the use of technology, a teacher who wants to use it but doesn't feel skilled enough, or a teacher who views it as an intrusion into your classroom. As schools look to instill complex skills that may be required of students in the future, school leadership is lauding the importance of technology (Project Tomorrow, 2017; 2016) and districts are increasingly adopting and implementing technology policies.

But the infusion of technology into classrooms has not been seamless for every teacher. Recall the statistics from the 2017 Speak Up survey—school technology leaders indicated that teachers were the greatest "challenge" to implementing digital learning and expanding technology toward more meaningful use with students (Project Tomorrow, 2017).

Importantly, teachers identified the supports they needed to integrate technology into instruction, including planning time, access to technology in the classroom, technology support, professional development, and reliable and high-quality Internet connectivity (Project Tomorrow, 2017).

The X framework and technology fitness rely squarely on the expertise of the teacher and respect their judgment regarding where and when technology is an appropriate curricular choice to infuse into practice. This book is not preaching to teachers about a new shiny "fix," but rather it offers a way to repurpose instructional practice in answer to some of the increasing demands of the classroom.

Instead of offering technology as a magical solution, consider it as one way, among many available to teachers, to repurpose practice. This perspective is based on two important ideas. The first, discussed in chapter 1, is the X framework, with the premise being that the combination of proactive teaching, universal design for learning, assistive technology, and self-reflection through technology fitness can create increased accessibility for more learners.

Other benefits include reducing the isolation of students who don't fit into the "middle," improved classroom community through the provision of increased and varied opportunities for engagement and expression, and efficient ways for educators to familiarize themselves with students' individual strengths and needs. This approach enhances teacher agency and makes technology an empowering addition to instructional practice, rather than an imposition posed by a school or district policy or a regulation.

The second idea is how to apply the X framework. Thus, in the pages that preceded this chapter, there are a variety of ideas for improving accessibility via the inclusion of technology in classroom practice. However, there are no fail-safe solutions to the realities of the classroom today, and technology changes rapidly, which is why the emphasis should be on building educators' skills and confidence to unpack, learn, and use novel technology instead of fixed skills around specific tools.

Repurposing practice requires time, patience, and commitment—much like any other effort. Remaining clear that technology is a way to repurpose rather than replace the existing expertise and efforts of the teacher will help to sustain educators through rapid shifts in "hot" technologies and fads that may be exciting but lack depth and breadth to help students learn critical thinking.

THE 20-60-20 RULE

It's also important to remember that everyone will approach classroom technology integration at their own pace. There's an often referred to organizational management principle called the 20-60-20 rule that suggests that people can be broadly categorized into three groups. It suggests that 20 percent of people are positive and forward thinking, even ahead of the curve with regard to new initiatives; 60 percent move with the community with support; and the final 20 percent require significant support—even persuasion—to propel them forward.

This is an interesting way to think about technology risk. However, a friendly revision to this principle might be to think about it as though it applies to every individual instead of a group. For example, sometimes a teacher might be eager to apply new technology, perhaps already tinkering with or trying out a given technology before receiving a complete explanation or overview. Other times—maybe most of the time—an educator could be interested or intrigued and possibly willing to try new technology, though usually requiring support.

Finally, there are times when an educator may be reticent about attempting to use a specific technology due to a range of different reasons, such as lack of confidence, bad experiences, disinterest, or mixed feelings about a particular technology's appropriateness or place in the classroom. Remember, technology knowledge does not necessarily equate to technology consumption or action, so at any time educators have the potential to repurpose their own practice and utilize technology in a way that suits them.

TECHNOLOGY AS FRIEND, NOT FOE

No matter what level of enthusiasm you might bring to a new initiative or classroom practice, getting started can be daunting. The first step to repurposing practice is to think about technology as a support rather than an encumbrance. Here's some encouragement to help you on your journey:

1. *Start somewhere, not everywhere.* Even the most sophisticated technology users would run screaming from their own classrooms if they attempted to do a technology overhaul of their practice. Using your technology fitness as a gauge, determine one place to start and build

your comfort level as you experience successes (and—be realistic— failures). It doesn't have to be a complete overhaul all at once—small steps are key in sustaining technology use. This is an excellent place to begin and ensures that you adopt practices that you can keep building on.

2. *Baby steps.* Sometimes technology seems more daunting than it really is because of the enormity of it. Break it down into small, concrete steps—baby steps! This builds confidence and encourages mastery of smaller, more manageable aspects of a new tech until you feel ready to take it on in its entirety. For example, perhaps you want to try using digital collaboration to capture ideas for the development of a class project. Instead of trying it all at once, try a smaller step: first have small groups use one document for real-time collaboration and practice until everyone, including you, gets comfortable with the technology.

3. *Find your people.* This is important advice for any aspect of professional practice but incredibly important for teachers who want to self-identify target areas for growth with technology. It's vital to align yourself with a group or a network—big or small—of likeminded educators with whom you can share ideas and progress and stay accountable to your own growth. It's also important to be able to decide on your own terms what technology you will use, how well it worked, and get feedback on why it did or did not help you to achieve the goals you identified. Your network can include technology users whose levels of expertise vary.

4. *Technology should make sense.* Yes, iPads are cool, and students love to use them. However, use should be compelled by a specific justification for their entrée into the classroom. This can be as simple as offering choices for expression or opportunities for creating similarities between students who require iPads to participate and students who might utilize them in one aspect of their learning.

    Any introduction of technology should have a clear curricular alignment. For example, if your goal is to improve classroom participation using technology, you'll have to use both short- and long-term data to answer your question in order to rule out the "bling effect." Who isn't at least momentarily intrigued with a shiny new device? To determine whether your choice actually improves participation, sustained opportunities for use may be necessary. However, you don't have to see participation skyrocket in order to create a justification for use—if the technology creates even one opportunity for a student to participate who typically would not have, it has a clear justification.

5. *Learning how to figure out and utilize a new technology is more important than what the technology du jour is.* There's a very simple

reason for this advice, because by the time you figure out that hot new app, device, interactive whiteboard, or program, another one likely will have been introduced or the technology will have evolved beyond it.

This might sound discouraging, but once you have a specific way to approach learning about and using something new, you can apply that method to other technologies. This can be accomplished by formalizing the "tinkering" method, the same one you might naturally use to become comfortable with a new phone or television—just trying it out and staying with it. What feels completely strange and unnatural at first soon feels like second nature (like driving a new car!). Figuring out the steps you personally take to feel comfortable with new technology will improve tech motivation and your willingness to take new technology risks. It will also help to operationalize your approach, or set a routine, thereby improving your comfort level about how you use tech.

6. *Practice makes . . . positive.* Practice hardly ever makes perfect, but it increases confidence and therefore willingness. Make using technology in the classroom a habit by trying to integrate it in a small way every single day. Tinker, tinker, tinker.

7. *Make notes.* This is extremely useful, especially at first. Use a notebook to jot down your reactions to using new technology. What went well? What did you feel at ease with? What do you need to practice more? Writing down the process helps you to identify the specific technology aspects with which you are most comfortable and to articulate to students, parents, and administrators why a particular technology is useful to instruction and how it can advance students' learning. It's also a great way to help you to pick up where you left off, and your notes might help a colleague in the future who wants to try what you are doing.

8. *Be uncomfortable.* Here's something really obvious: things feel difficult when you're outside of your comfort zone. But if it were easy, you would already know how to do it. When you're struggling, it's often because you're on the cusp of learning something new. The frustration you feel is your brain working to integrate the knowledge in a way that makes sense for you. So remember, success is often just beyond the frustration. Be willing to be uncomfortable—teachers ask students to do this on an almost daily basis! Encourage yourself the way you might encourage your students.

9. *Technology fails—sometimes as often as it works.* This is the most obvious but also most important advice to consider when integrating the use of technology into teaching practice. Years ago, people memorized phone numbers because they needed to. Today, phones store

your numbers and even dial them for you, so there's less need for memorization. However, batteries die, phones break, and emergencies happen. We still need backups, no matter how convenient technology can be. So it's important to have a plan B when first implementing a new technology in the classroom. This provides a great opportunity for your students as well: modeling how to respond to failure is as important a lesson as any, so even when technology fails, it remains an effective teaching tool in the classroom.

10. *Keep trying.* There's no end point to your technology growth. You can keep trying, learning, growing as you try new things—some of which will work for you and some which won't. Using technology can improve access for students who are struggling and create new opportunities for engagement for all students. The important thing to remember is that there's no one specific or "right" way to use tech, only the way that is right for your classroom.

At the end of the (school) day, there's no one better than you to decide what tools complement your instruction and what tools you should use in your classroom. Technology is merely a vehicle to learning, and educators do need to guard against using it without purpose. The key to effective technology use is in finding the balance for yourself and recognizing that it will not be the same for every educator.

Remember that when used incorrectly, technology can frustrate both teachers and students. But when used correctly, it can create openings for students to engage, participate, and access knowledge that they otherwise might not have, and it can enhance your instruction such that it's less—not more—work. Rely on your own expertise to determine what level is appropriate for your practice. There always will be evolving technology, shifting philosophies, and new ideas, but nothing will ever replace the true expert— the teacher.

References

American Federation of Teachers & Badass Teachers Association (2015). Quality of worklife survey. Retrieved June 21, 2017, from www.aft.org/sites/default/files/worklifesurveyresults2015.pdf.

Armbruster, P., Patel, M., Johnson, E., & Weiss, M. (2009). Active learning and student-centered pedagogy improve student attitudes and performance in introductory biology. *CBE–Life Sciences Education, 8*(3), 203–13.

Bergmann, J., & Sams, A. (2012). Flip your classroom: Reach every student in every class every day. International Society for Technology in Education.

Bevan, B., Gutwill, J. P., Petrich, M., & Wilkinson, K. (2015). Learning through STEM-rich tinkering: Findings from a jointly negotiated research project taken up in practice. *Science Education, 99*(1), 98–120.

Bitterman, N., & Shalev, I. (2004). The silver surfer: Making the internet usable for seniors. *Ergonomics in Design, 12*(1), 24–28.

Bowler, L. (2014). Creativity through "maker" experiences and design thinking in the education of librarians. *Knowledge Quest, 40*(5).

Carlson, D., Ehrlich, N., Berland, B., & Bailey, N. (2001). Assistive technology survey results: Continued benefits and needs reported by Americans with disabilities. *Research Exchange, 7*(1).

Carnevale, A. P. (2001). Help wanted . . . College required. Washington, DC: Educational Testing Service, Office for Public Leadership.

Carnoy, M., & Rothstein, R. (2013). What do international tests really show about US student performance? *Economic Policy Institute, 28*, 32–33.

CAST. (2011). *Universal Design for Learning Guidelines version 2.0.* Wakefield, MA: Center for Applied Special Technology.

CAST (2014). *What is universal design for learning?* Wakefield, MA: Center for Applied Special Technology. Retrieved from http://www.udlcenter.org/aboutudl/whatisudl.

Cochran-Smith, M., Baker, M., Burton, S., Chang, W. C., Fernandez, M. B., Keefe, E. S., Miller, A., Sanchez, J. G., Stern, R. (2017). Teacher quality and teacher education policy: The U.S. case and its implications. In M. Akiba & G. LeTendre, (Eds.), *Routledge international handbook of teacher quality and policy.* New York: Routledge.

Cochran-Smith, M., Baker, M., Burton, S., Chang, W. C., Fernandez, M. B., Keefe, E. S., Miller, A., Sanchez, J. G. (in press). *Reclaiming accountability: Teacher education in uncertain times.* New York: Teacher's College Press.

Cochran-Smith, M., Stern, R., Sánchez, J. G., Miller, A., Keefe, E. S., Fernández, B., Chang, W-C., Carney, M., Burton, S., & Baker, M. (2016). *Holding teacher education accountable: A review of claims and evidence.* Boulder, CO: National Education Policy Center.

Corno, L. Y. N. (2008). On teaching adaptively. *Educational Psychologist, 43*(3), 161–73.

De Arment, S. T., Reed, E., & Wetzel, A. P. (2013). Promoting adaptive expertise: A conceptual framework for special educator preparation. *Teacher Education and Special Education, 36*(3), 217–30.

Dougherty, D. (2012). The maker movement. *Innovations, 7*(3), 11–14.

Edyburn, D. L. (2000). Assistive technology and students with mild disabilities. *Focus on Exceptional Children, 32*(9), 1.

Edyburn, D. L. (2005). Assistive technology and students with mild disabilities: From consideration to outcome measurement. *Handbook of special education technology research and practice*, 239–70.

Edyburn, D. L. (2006). Assistive technology and mild disabilities. *Special Education Technology Practice, 8*(4), 18–28.

Edyburn, D. L. (2010). Would you recognize universal design for learning if you saw it? Ten propositions for new directions for the second decade of UDL. *Learning Disability Quarterly, 33*(1), 33–41.

Edyburn, D., Higgins, K., & Boone, R. (2005). *Handbook of special education technology research and practice*. Whitefish Bay, WI: Knowledge by Design.

Family Center on Technology and Disability. (2008). Preservice AT training: Infusion is the word. *News and Notes, 73*, 3–14. Retrieved from www.fctd.info/assets/newsletters/pdfs/255/FCTD_Apr08_Issue73.pdf?1209535200.

File, T. (2013). Computer and internet use in the United States. Current Population Survey Reports, P20-568. U.S. Census Bureau, Washington, DC.

Fleming, L. (2015). *Worlds of making: Best practices for establishing a makerspace in your school.* Thousand Oaks, CA: Corwin Press.

Forgrave, K. E. (2002). Assistive technology: Empowering students with learning disabilities. *The Clearing House, 75*(3), 122–26.

Freeman, S., Eddy, S. L., McDonough, M., Smith, M. K., Okoroafor, N., Jordt, H., & Wenderoth, M. P. (2014). Active learning increases student performance in science, engineering, and mathematics. *Proceedings of the National Academy of Sciences, 111*(23), 8410–15.

Ginsburg, K. (2007). The importance of play in promoting healthy child development and maintaining strong parent-child bonds. *Pediatrics, 119* (1).

Hammerness, K., Darling-Hammond, L., & Bransford, J. (2005). How teachers learn and develop. In L. Darling-Hammond & J. Bransford, (Eds.), *Preparing teachers for a changing world: What teacher should learn and be able to do*, pp. 358–89. San Francisco, CA: Wiley & Sons.

Hargreaves, A., & Braun, H. (2012). Leading for all: A research report of the development, design, implementation and impact of Ontario's "Essential for Some, Good for All" initiative. Ontario, Canada: Council of Ontario Directors of Education.

Hashey, A. I., & Stahl, S. (2014). Making online learning accessible for students with disabilities. *Teaching Exceptional Children, 46*(5), 70–78.

Individuals with Disabilities Education Act, 20 U.S.C. § 1400 (2004).

Jackson, R. M., & Karger, J. (2015). Audio-supported reading and students with learning disabilities. Wakefield, MA: National Center on Accessible Educational Materials. Retrieved from http://aem.cast.org/about/publications/2015/audio-supported-reading-learning-disabilities-asr-ld.html.

Johnson, D., Thurlow, M., & Schuelka, M. (2012). Diploma options, graduation requirements, and exit exams for youth with disabilities: 2011 national study. Minneapolis, MN: National Center on Educational Outcomes.

Johnson, D. W., & Johnson, R. (1999). Learning together and alone: Cooperative, competitive, and individualistic learning (5th Ed.). Boston: Allyn & Bacon.

King, A. (1993). From sage on the stage to guide on the side. *College Teaching, 41*(1).

King-Sears, M. (2009). Universal design for learning: Technology and pedagogy. *Learning Disability Quarterly, 32*(4), 199–201.

Lei, J., & Zhao, Y. (2008). One-to-one computing: What does it bring to schools? *Journal of Educational Computing Research, 39*(2), 97–122.

Lenhart, A. (2015). Teen, social media and technology overview 2015. Washington, DC: Pew Research Center.

Lewis, R. B. (1998). Assistive technology and learning disabilities: Today's realities and tomorrow's promises. *Journal of Learning Disabilities, 31*(1), 16–26.

Losen, D. & Gillespie, J. (2012). Opportunities suspended: The disparate impact of disciplinary exclusion from school. Los Angeles: The Civil Rights Project at UCLA.

Massachusetts Department of Elementary and Secondary Education. (2011). Massachusetts curriculum framework for English language arts and literacy. Retrieved July 21, 2016, from www.doe.mass.edu/frameworks/current.html.

Meyer, A., Rose, D. H., & Gordon, D. T. (2014). *Universal design for learning: Theory and practice.* Wakefield, MA: CAST Professional Publishing.

Mishra, P., & Koehler, M. J. (2006). Technological pedagogical content knowledge: A framework for teacher knowledge. *Teachers College Record, 108*(6), 1017.

Morrison, K. (2007). Implementation of assistive computer technology: A model for school systems. *International Journal of Special Education, 22*(1), 83–95.

Mull, C. A., & Sitlington, P. L. (2003). The role of technology in the transition to postsecondary education of students with learning disabilities: A review of the literature. *The Journal of Special Education, 37*(1), 26–32.

National Academy of Science. (2015). Mental disorders and disabilities among low income children. Washington, DC: The National Academies Press.

National Association of Special Education Teachers. (n.d.). Characteristics of children with learning disabilities. Retrieved August 1, 2017, from www.naset.org/fileadmin/user_upload/LD_Report/Issue__3_LD_Report_Characteristic_of_LD.pdf.

National Center for Education Statistics. (2015). ED*Facts* data groups 695 and 696, school year 2013–2014; September 4, 2015. Retrieved August 25, 2017, from https://nces.ed.gov/ccd/tables/ACGR_RE_and_characteristics_2013-14.asp.

Norris, P. (2001). *Digital divide: Civic engagement, information poverty, and the Internet worldwide.* Cambridge: Cambridge University Press.

Parette, P., & Scherer, M. (2004). Assistive technology use and stigma. *Education and Training in Developmental Disabilities, 39*(3), 217–26.

Penuel, W. R. (2006). Implementation and effects of one-to-one computing initiatives: A research synthesis. *Journal of Research on Technology in Education, 38*(3), 329–48.

Perrin, A. (2015). Social media usage. *Pew Research Center.*

Project Tomorrow. (2016). 2016 Digital learning reports from Blackboard and Speak Up. Retrieved May 1, 2017, from www.tomorrow.org/speakup/2016-digital-learning-reports-from-blackboard-and-speak-up.html.

Project Tomorrow. (2017). Trends in digital learning: Building teachers' capacity and competency to create new learning experiences for students. Retrieved August 1, 2017, from www.tomorrow.org/speakup/speak-up-2016-trends-digital-learning-june-2017.html.

Riemer-Reiss, M. L., & Wacker, R. R. (1999). Assistive technology use and abandonment among college students with disabilities. *International Electronic Journal for Leadership in Learning, 3,* (23).

Rose, D. H., Hasselbring, T. S., Stahl, S., & Zabala, J. (2005). Assistive technology and universal design for learning: Two sides of the same coin. In D. Edyburn, K. Higgins, & R. Boone (Eds.), *Handbook of special education technology research and practice,* pp. 507–18. Oviedo, FL: Knowledge by Design.

Rose, D. H., & Meyer, A. (2002). *Teaching every student in the digital age: Universal design for learning.* Alexandria, VA: Association for Supervision and Curriculum Development.

Sawyer, R. J., Graham, S., & Harris, K. R. (1992). Direct teaching, strategy instruction, and strategy instruction with explicit self-regulation: Effects on the composition skills and self-efficacy of students with learning disabilities. *Journal of educational psychology, 84*(3), 340.

Smith, A. (2017). Record shares of Americans now own smartphones, have home broadband. Pew Research Center. Retrieved from www.pewresearch.org/fact-tank/2017/01/12/evolution-of-technology/.

Staker, H., & Horn, M. B. (2012). Classifying K–12 blended learning. Innosight Institute. Retrieved from www.christenseninstitute.org/wp-content/uploads/2013/04/Classifying-K-12-blended-learning.pdf.

Statistic Brain. (2017). New Year's resolution statistics. Retrieved from www.statisticbrain.com/new-years-resolution-statistics.

Steiner, A. (2017). The impact of a one to one laptop program on the self-efficacy of middle school students with specific learning disabilities. Retrieved from http://hdl.handle.net/2345/bc-ir:107567.

Sugai, G., Horner, R. H., Dunlap, G., Hieneman, M., Lewis, T. J., Nelson, C. M., Scott, T., Liaupsin, C., Sailor, W., Turnbull, A. P., Turnbull, H. R., III, Wickham, D., Reuf, M., & Wilcox, B. (2000). Applying positive behavioral support and functional behavioral assessment in schools. *Journal of Positive Behavioral Interventions, 2*, 131–43.

Sugai, G., Horner, R. H., & Gresham, F. (2002). Behaviorally effective school environments. In M. R. Shinn, G. Stoner, & H. M. Walker (Eds.), *Interventions for academic and behavior problems: Preventive and remedial approaches* (pp. 315–50). Silver Spring, MD: National Association of School Psychologists.

Thurlow, M., & Johnson, D. (2011). The high school dropout dilemma and special education students. California Dropout Research Project, Policy Brief 18. Retrieved August 10, 2017, from http://cdrpsb.org/pubs_reports.htm.

Tierney, J. (2013). The coming revolution in public education. *The Atlantic*. Retrieved June 22, 2015, from www.theatlantic.com/national/archive/2013/04/the-coming-revolution-in-public-education/275163.

Todis, B. (1996). Tools for the task? Perspectives on assistive technology in educational settings. *Journal of Special Education Technology, 13*, 49–61.

Warschauer, M., Zheng, B., Niiya, M., Cotten, S., & Farkas, G. (2014). Balancing the one-to-one equation: Equity and access in three laptop programs. *Equity & Excellence in Education, 47*(1), 46–62.

Westheimer, J. (2008). No child left thinking: Democracy at risk in American schools. *Colleagues, 3*(2). Retrieved June 24, 2015 from http://scholarworks.gvsu.edu/colleagues/vol3/iss2/8.

Zimmerman, B. J. (2000). Self-efficacy: An essential motive to learn. *Contemporary Educational Psychology, 25*, 82–91.

About the Authors

Elizabeth Stringer Keefe is a teacher educator and researcher at the Graduate School of Education, Lesley University, in Cambridge, Massachusetts. Her work and research at the university focus on special education teacher preparation, particularly in the area of autism. She is a member of Project TEER, an international multidisciplinary research team of eight teacher education scholars and practitioners who research education reform policy and accountability mechanisms in teacher education. Elizabeth has more than twenty years of experience in public and private education settings, as a teacher, consultant, and critical friend to various nonprofits. She is president of Massachusetts Council for Exceptional Children and a member of Massachusetts Advocates for Children Autism Center Advisory Board. Elizabeth lives in Bedford, Massachusetts, with her husband, Dennis, three energetic, creative, and technologically adept young children, Lucy, Cam, and Cooper, and their aging and beloved dog, Zoe.

Adam Steiner is a technology integration specialist for Holliston Public Schools in Holliston, Massachusetts, and recently completed a PhD at Boston College with a focus on curriculum, instruction, and technology. His research interests include one-to-one technology, universal design, and educational change. Prior to becoming a technology integration specialist, Adam was a high school social studies teacher for ten years. Adam is a board member of Massachusetts Council for Exceptional Children and a long-serving member of Framingham Town Meeting. He lives in Framingham with his wife and two daughters.

Lightning Source UK Ltd.
Milton Keynes UK
UKHW010028100419

340779UK00007B/219/P